What a wonderful delight to see a book published that discusses an area of life in which satan has had a field day and played havoc, to the demise of many couples—marriage and the family. Divorce rates are escalating; legal separations are occurring on a daily basis. White collar and blue collar, professional and layperson, Christian and non-Christian alike are walking away from their spouses and homes without even looking back—many times because they were never prepared for marriage and the family in the first place. That's why this book, *Crazy House, Sane House,* is so important. The Bloomers are a delightful couple with many years of marital experience. Incorporating wisdom with wonderful humor, they express a sincere desire to see that men and women become equipped to build and sustain the insititution so sacred to God— marriage and the family. You may laugh, and you may cry, but you will indentify with the practical truths and principles shared in this book.

—Dr. Wanda A. Turner,
Author of *Even with My Issues,*
Pastor of Covenant Worship Center,
Inglewood, California

Crazy House

SANE HOUSE

Crazy House

SANE HOUSE

GEORGE & JEANNIE BLOOMER

ய

WHITAKER
HOUSE

CRAZY HOUSE, SANE HOUSE

G. G. Bloomer Ministries
515 Dowd St.
Durham, NC 27701

ISBN: 0-88368-726-7
Printed in the United States of America
© 2001 by George & Jeannie Bloomer

Whitaker House
30 Hunt Valley Circle
New Kensington, PA 15068

Library of Congress Cataloging-in-Publication Data

Bloomer, George G., 1963–
  Crazy house, sane house / George & Jeannie Bloomer.
    p. cm.
  ISBN 0-88368-726-7 (pbk. : alk. paper)
  1. Marriage—Religious aspects—Christianity. I. Bloomer, Jeannie, 1965– II. Title.
  BV835 .B58 2002
  248.4—dc21   2001007530

1 2 3 4 5 6 7 8 9 10 11 12 / 10 09 08 07 06 05 04 03 02

CONTENTS

INTRODUCTION

WHAT ARE YOU BUILDING?

Imagine that one morning I wake up and decide to build a new house. So, filled with the anticipation of building and owning something, I drive down to the bank and ask to speak to someone in the loan department. They gladly lead me to the desk and smiling face of a loan officer at the bank, and a conversation ensues that goes something like this...

"Hello, Pastor Bloomer. My name is Mrs. Smith of the Sovereign National Union of Banks (SNUB). We here at SNUB are committed to giving you our business any way we can. Now, how can I help you?"

"I would like to build a new house, and I need a loan."

"Great! We would be happy to help you. That's why we're here. Let's just take a few minutes to fill out some information on this loan application. Now, what kind of

9

house would you like to build? How much money will you need? Where would you like to build the house? What kind of a down payment do you have? What kind of mortgage payment can you afford? Who will you contract to build your new home?"

"Whew! I didn't think of all that stuff. Do I really need to know all that before I build a house? Why can't you just call the lumberyard and ask them to send over some concrete blocks, lumber, windows, and stuff like that? I'll let you know when I run out of money and materials and call you back for some more. Okay?"

Sounds silly, doesn't it? We would never think of going to a bank and asking for thousands of dollars to build a house without knowing what we wanted to build! We have to produce a building plan and prove the value of the investment the bank would be making. Nevertheless, many people enter into the serious business of marriage in just as haphazard a way as I've described above. People believe that somehow, in some way, everything will just come together. That makes about as much sense as going to the bank and asking them to pay for some odds and ends of stuff with which to build a new house that we can't even describe to them. If we have no idea what we are building, we will end up with what I call a "crazy house."

There is a growing community of young people in our nation who are victims of single-parent or divorced homes and who therefore seek to have a relationship without marriage. They have no trust in the institution of marriage because they were caught in the cross fire of unsound relationships. Many believe that just living together, or "shacking up," is better than getting married. They are settling for live-in lovers instead of entering the sanctity of matrimony—which provides the legal and spiritual covering they need.

Marriage is a covenant that God created to help establish unity and harmony in the earth. But marriage requires two people who are willing to work at keeping it. If one party wants to work at it and the other one doesn't, then the marriage has already failed.

> MARRIAGE IS A COV-
> ENANT THAT GOD
> CREATED TO HELP
> ESTABLISH UNITY
> AND HARMONY IN
> THE EARTH.

Marriage is the coming together of two people who desire to build something of eternal value that brings glory to God. Marriages sometimes fall apart because the partners have no clear vision, no understanding of what is expected of each of them. Each spouse sees the other as some kind of household appliance meant to meet his or her needs rather than a partner with whom he or she is building a lifelong, "till death do us part" kind of enterprise.

In marriage two people invest in each other without any expectation of a particular dividend. Marriage is motivated by mutual servanthood and held together by the grace of God—and grace is needed at every turn. There's no such thing as a perfect marriage—a marriage in which everything just somehow comes together without mutual investment. No, everybody must work on it. Both partners must give in order to get, and both must invest everything and not hold back anything if they are to bring glory to God through their marriage.

Many people live under the false assumption that if problems arise, it means that the marriage is not working. That's not so. After many years of marriage, my wife and I have come to understand that trials will come, and that when they do there is a master plan we can refer to that will help us get back on track. So, just as we have built our marriage together, my wife and I have written this book together. Some of what we have included here is just common sense. Other parts may stretch you a bit. But all of it is based on our own experience, sometimes expressed in brutal honesty. And if you will read and take heed, dear readers, you are the ones who will reap the rewards of our investments and mistakes.

Since married partners are, in fact, building something, we employ some of the same terms you might use if you were to build a house. With that in mind, there are two phases to this construction: laying the foundations and building the house. By following the principles for each phase, you will make the difference in the final product you build. It will make the difference between a *crazy house* and a *sane house*.

REMARKS FROM JEANNIE BLOOMER

Many of us spend a lot of time and resources beautifying our homes. For most of us, our homes are the biggest monetary investment that we will make in our lives. And just as we build strong and solid houses out of good materials in order to avoid weakness and possible collapse, so should we build strong households with the solid material of the Bible and the grace to guard against the stresses that can bring them down in a heap. The storms of life will beat upon the structure of our marriage and families. We must be wise concerning the devices of the enemy and protect, appreciate, and maintain that which no man can put asunder.

Balance is an integral part of every marriage. There has to be a balance of roles in the house between husband and wife, as well as a balance of mercy and trust upon which the house is established. A wise house is a sane house. A wise house builder knows there is a plan to follow and an objective to be achieved. Without a plan, we build houses that are destined to crumble under the weight of everyday life and the normal crises that face any marriage. We cannot just build any way we choose and hope to arrive at a stable house. *"For every house is builded by some man; but he that built all things is God"* (Hebrews 3:4 KJV). The strongest material we can use as our foundation is the wisdom and knowledge of God.

Marriage is not a dictatorship, where one spouse spills out orders while the other unwillingly acquiesces to "authority." Instead, a sane house is built with an understanding and respect for the other partner within the house. The houses we are building will experience shifting and change that require a strong foundation laid with the materials of honesty, confrontation, trust, loyalty, protection, and commitment. When the foundations and materials are good, our houses can withstand even the toughest gales and winds.

Marriage is not without its struggles, but a marriage committed to working through the seemingly rough times is a marriage destined to make it through to see the good times. My husband and I are proud to open our household and share our struggles with you. Our adjustments, our trials, and even our victories as described in *Crazy House, Sane House* are true accounts of a marriage tested by trial and established on faith. We hope that this book will be an encouragement to you as you build or perhaps remodel your own house, standing on the promises you've made to God and each other. Though your marriage will never be problem-free, you will be free to deal wisely with those problems when they come.

> IF YOU ARE COM-
> MITTED TO WORKING
> THROUGH ROUGH
> TIMES, YOU ARE DES-
> TINED TO SEE THE
> GOOD TIMES.

PART ONE

LAYING THE FOUNDATION

CHAPTER ONE

BLUEPRINTS FOR A SANE HOUSE

CHAPTER ONE

BLUEPRINTS FOR A SANE HOUSE

WHAT KIND OF HOUSE DO YOU SEE?

Many times we hear people say of marriage, "It just didn't turn out the way I planned." Perhaps they got married because of an emotional or hormonal response to someone of the opposite gender. Or maybe they got married so that they could have sex without guilt. Either way, they really never gave any serious thought to what it means to be married. They got married without any purpose or vision.

Anything we do without purpose or vision is doomed to fail. Purpose gives reason for a person or thing to exist. Purpose literally means "stepping forward" toward an objective.* For example, when you get into

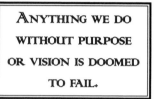

ANYTHING WE DO WITHOUT PURPOSE OR VISION IS DOOMED TO FAIL.

your car, you have a purpose, even if it's just to go for a ride. If you need to get something from the grocery store, you write a list of what is needed, and then you get into the car and drive to the store. In that case, your purpose is to fill your belly. The list is a vision statement of how you will fulfill that purpose. Purpose, then, gives us the reason we do something, and vision provides a picture that we can see as we move toward that purpose. So, when people say that things didn't turn out the way they planned, they aren't telling the whole truth. Things probably turned out exactly the way they planned—which is not at all!

Before we begin to build anything, we must have a vision of what we want to build. When we decide to build a house, we go to a builder, and he shows us several floor plans and options from which we design our new house. (These days some builders even have computer programs that let us build a "virtual house" by putting together several options—how many bedrooms, what kind of windows, and so on.) Once we have an idea of what we want, the builder or architect produces a set of blueprints. These blueprints capture the vision in our hearts in great detail so that we can

* *The American Heritage® Dictionary of the English Language,* 3rd edition, © 1996 by Houghton Mifflin Company. Electronic version licensed from INSO Corporation.

actually *see* what our house will look like when it is finished. That *seeing* is our vision. The same principle holds true with a marriage. We must know the purpose for which we have gotten married and have a vision to aim at. What kind of marriage do we see? What kind of marriage does God see?

THE MARRIAGE THAT GOD SEES

God's vision for marriage is simple and direct.

> *Therefore a man shall leave his father and mother and be joined to his wife, and they shall become one flesh.* (Genesis 2:24)

God's vision of marriage is that two become one flesh. Being *"one flesh"* means that the two who got married are one in purpose and vision. Marriage is oneness, pure and simple. God sees two people who are united into one new person, with each partner completing the other. God

> MARRIAGE IS ONE-
> NESS, PURE AND
> SIMPLE.

used the word for *one* that also means "first." Whatever and whoever we were before we got married, now the marriage comes first. But before the two can become one, there must be a "leaving" and a "cleaving."

LEAVING

We are to "leave" all other influences and purposes behind and "cleave" to our spouse. To leave means that we break loose of all former expectations and live totally within the marriage. Did you ever notice how many times God told people to leave where they were in order to go where He wanted to take them? God told Abram that he had to leave his country, his family, and his father's house. (See Genesis 12:1.) In other words, Abram would not be able to carry his *culture*, his *customs*, or his *comfort* with him into the new place God promised to him. Neither can we carry any of these into our marriages. It was the same with Moses, who had to leave the seclusion of Goshen to deliver a people. It was the same with the youngest son of Jesse; he had to leave the sheep in the fields and go giant-killing. We cannot stay were we are and get to where God is taking us in ministry or in our marriage.

Some of these influences and purposes may come from the home or the culture in which we grew up. There are a million and more things that can tear a marriage apart if we allow them to. Some of these things can be as simple as where you will eat Thanksgiving dinner. We humans tend to get so accustomed to certain standards and traditions. Before we got married, we took it for granted that when we opened the cupboard we would find food—and everyone knows to put the cap back on the toothpaste! But all those comforts and assumptions go out the window when we get married. Customs must give way to compromise; traditions become trade-offs, and comforts yield to mutual accommodation.

A person who comes from an affluent family will find it difficult to understand why he can't buy a brand-new car every year, or why she can't take off on a European vacation. Such individuals will ask, "Why is this happening to me?" They see as a hardship what is just a fact of life—that it takes time to establish a financial position. Even those who have grown up with the experience of having the electricity or water cut off because the bill wasn't paid can grow resentful of financial challenges within a marriage. They thought that the simple act of saying "I do" would bring their bad financial habits to an end. It's just not that easy. The truth is that things like personal finances and bad spending habits need to be addressed *before* we plan the honeymoon. The sun is going to rise on the day after our wedding, and somebody is going to have to pay the hotel bill.

When reality hits us and we find that somebody packed problems along with our wedding gifts, we begin the blame game. The new wife living in the new environment of marriage begins to complain, while the husband asks, "What's wrong with this woman? I'm doing all I can to take care of her and keep a roof over her head, yet she nags me to death as soon as I come through the door!" Then the wife says that Daddy took care of everything: "My daddy did this, and my daddy did that...." I think of my teenage daughter, Jessica. The man whom she marries will really have to have the means and the mind to take good care of her. She's used to having the things that she needs, or the things that she wants, so she may not have the patience to deal with a man who does not provide for her. They both will need to know what the other expects and establish their own vision for their marriage.

Jeannie: The mistake that many young people make is to marry without getting to know each other or learning anything about running a household. This was the case with our marriage. George and I married at a very young age—we were just twenty and eighteen. So, of course, we didn't know each other all that well. All we knew was that we were in love, and that was enough. If we had known then what we know now, we could have bypassed much of the turmoil that our marriage experienced in its earlier stages. But by the grace of God we are still together and thriving.

Planning and communicating before marriage are so important. Both parties must get to know each other before making that final commitment of marriage. Even now I often ask my husband, "How are you doing? Is there anything new going on that I need to know?" This is the way we keep moving toward our vision for our marriage. It is too easy to grow apart from each other. We will never know what our marriage partner thinks unless we ask him or her. Communication is extremely important in a marriage.

Bishop: Of course, all marriages will be tested, but couples who get to know each other stand a better chance of passing the tests. So take time to know the person with whom you plan to make such an important and lifelong commitment.

CLEAVING

And he answered and said unto them, Have ye not read, that he which made them at the beginning made them male and female, and said, For this cause shall a man leave father and mother, and shall cleave to his wife: and they twain shall be one flesh? Wherefore they are no more

twain, but one flesh. What therefore God hath joined together, let no man put asunder
(Matthew 19:4–6 KJV)

Not only do we need to break the bonds of the culture, customs, and comfort of our former families, but we also must become glued or bonded to our spouse and form a new culture with new customs and new comfort. The Bible calls this "cleaving." To cleave means that we become inseparably joined to one another. The Hebrew word actually refers to something glued together that no man can tear apart. But this bonding cannot take place until both parties break old bonds and give themselves unreservedly to the new bonding.

Cleaving also means that we begin to live for our marriage partner. Of course, we cannot do this if we don't have a sense of calling in the bonds of marriage. What do I mean by that? In one sense, we are called to be God's vessel of ministry to the other partner; we are God's chosen vessel of ministry to meet his or her needs. However, we cannot give ourselves to the calling of God in marriage if we do not trust that He has called us. Let me be real here and say that none of us can do this in our own power. We are all still becoming more like Jesus. But when the calling of God puts us together, the grace of God keeps us together. God becomes the glue that holds us together.

Jesus added some clarity regarding marriage in the Gospel passage quoted earlier. He said that not only do we need to be *"one flesh"*—having the same vision and purpose—but we also must understand that no one else should try to interfere or distort that vision. Marriage is God's business. It was God who joined the parties together, and no one else has the right to get into God's business. Jesus was not just talking about someone encouraging another person to divorce or separate; He was talking about keeping the bounds and vision of marriage sanctified. We did not marry our parents or our friends. We married each other before God and for His glory.

It is important to keep private things private and not violate the trust between us as couples. We should never discuss personal marital issues with others except in extreme cases such as abuse or during marital counseling. Outsiders who gain knowledge of a couple's difficulties are rarely objective in the counsel they give. For example, it would not be good for the husband to complain to his mother about his wife's pot roast. Naturally, no one can make that dish like Mom, and Mom has no grace to give the woman who took her son. The vision for the marriage is the sole property and domain of those within the marriage and is no one else's business. God binds us together so that no one else can come between us.

WHAT DO YOU SEE?

What do you see in your marriage? Perhaps you have been married for a while but still have no clear vision of what you are building together. Maybe the house you started to build looks different from what you expected.

It probably looks a lot different from the one your parents built—and maybe it's better. Even if you have not drawn up the blueprint for your marriage, it's not too late.

Go to the One who called you together, and start there. God called you together in this cooperative venture to bring glory to Himself. Your marriage is a window to heaven through which others see God. So go to Him and see if you need to start working on some of the foundations for your house. Remember:

- Anything built without purpose and vision is doomed to fail.

- Marriage is a calling to be one in purpose and vision.

- You cannot stay where you are and respond to the calling of God.

- God has called you together to bring glory to Him.

CHAPTER TWO

COURTSHIP: BUILDING
ON A SOLID BASE

COURTSHIP: BUILDING ON A SOLID BASE

ARE YOU BUILDING YOUR HOUSE ON SAND OR SOLID ROCK?

One of the foundation stones of marriage missing in today's culture is the principle of courtship. Today's culture has replaced the act of courting a prospective spouse—someone with whom we would spend the rest of our lives—with dating. This is an ungodly idea of courtship. Now, there is nothing wrong with dating itself, but the spirit behind it is more carnal than spiritual. Because dating is based on superficial concerns and never crosses over into the spiritual realm, today we have marriages that are superficial and not spiritual. Many of these marriages are doomed to fail.

If we are going to build something that will last, we must build it on a solid base. Why? The base upon

> ALL THAT IS FIRM AND SOLID ON OUR WEDDING DAY WILL SHIFT AND SETTLE A LITTLE LOWER AS THE YEARS ROLL ON.

which we build will determine the ability of our house to withstand the storms that will come. Remember the fool who built his house on sand and the wise man who built his on the rock? (See Matthew 7:24–27.) Jesus, of course, is the Rock upon which we establish our marriage and family. We build our house on our knowledge of Jesus Christ. But some people choose to build on the sandy instability of physical appearance, which will shift as certainly as the sand of the sea. All that is firm and solid on our wedding day will shift and settle a little lower as the years roll on.

Another stone in the solid base of marriage is the knowledge of the one you intend to marry. What we mean here is knowledge of more than just superficial things, such as how a person looks or what kind of food he or she likes. We are talking about a deep knowledge of the other person. What is his relationship to God? What kind of family background does she have? We need to know about finances and a host of other practical things. Unfortunately, we seldom address any of these in today's climate of biological infatuation.

Society's idea of courtship today is more like test driving a new car than connecting with a mate on a deep spiritual level. The family is seldom involved in the process, and the emphasis is on physical compatibility and pleasure. The way we "shop" for a spouse isn't much different from the way we shop for a new car. When we buy a car, we look at the paint job and take it for a ride to see how it handles. If we drive it around

> TODAY, COURTSHIP IS MORE LIKE TEST DRIVING A CAR THAN CONNECTING WITH A MATE ON A SPIRITUAL LEVEL.

for a while and then decide that we don't like it, we just return it to the car dealership and move on down the road. We approach courting the same way. Many people are going out for too many test drives. The problem is that people are not cars; they cannot be returned so easily.

Today we see boys and girls at younger and younger ages hanging all over each other in public places and becoming intimate in private places. We have children having children. The approach the schools take is to talk about how to have sex so as to not contract a disease or get pregnant. They call it "safe sex." The Bible calls it fornication. In reality there is no such thing as safe sex. Sexual intimacy is powerful. It's awesome. It is the power of procreation through which future generations are released. It is not meant to be a hobby. Sadly, our society makes light of it, stripping it of all its great power and mystery. The message our young folks get is that it's just a biological urge to be obeyed carefully. God intended none of these things.

As a result, courtship is one of the most important issues in marriage. In the previous chapter, we talked about having a vision for marriage. That vision comes about as the result of courtship. You see, biblical courtship is more than dating. It is a process of preparation for both future husband and future wife that involves counsel and leadership by both the parents and the church. The parents and the church support each other in guiding and preparing the ones who are getting married.

BIBLICAL COURTSHIP

The contemporary practice of "test driving" potential mates was unknown in the Bible. In Bible times, marriage was taken more seriously; it was a covenant relationship between a man and a woman. Both the family and the community played major roles in this courtship.

In biblical times, two people intending to marry went through a period of "betrothal" that could have lasted a year or more. This was the case with Joseph and Mary, the earthly parents of Jesus. The betrothal was taken so seriously by the family and the whole village that it could not be broken by less than a certificate of divorce. It was a time of preparation and of building relationships. Today, however, dating is a casual matter from which most parents and pastors are excluded. The results are tragic, with soaring divorce rates and pre-marital sex a given even among Christian families.

During the time of betrothal, the prospective groom was to prepare a place—a home—for his future wife. It was his responsibility to make sure that things were secure financially. How many dads today sit down with future sons-in-law to ask about their finances? That young man dating our daughter will someday be the father of our grandchildren. How do we want those children to grow up? As parents, we have the right to know something about those young men our daughters see. We have the responsibility to know where they are spiritually, financially, and every other way.

At the same time, while the young man was preparing a place for his betrothed, the bride-to-be was preparing herself for marriage at the direction of her parents. She was learning about running a household. How many young women today know anything about running a home? Of course, the world is trying to get them out of the home and into the workplace. Still, if there is anyone who can keep the bride-to-be accountable, it is her mother or another older woman who can act as a mentor. In both cases, for both the prospective bride and the future groom, the parents need to get involved in setting the standards of righteousness for courtship.

THE RESPONSIBILITY OF PARENTS AND THE CHURCH IN COURTSHIP

When it comes to dating and relationships between our teens, moms and dads should be in the loop. Why? First of all, they themselves were subject to some of the same temptations and issues perhaps only fifteen or twenty years before. Moms and dads can recognize the potential traps that their children can fall into, and they can help to keep both parties accountable. Although we can't prevent every young person from getting pregnant or from becoming too emotionally involved in relationships at too young an age, we can provide guidance, and we can trust that we have instilled righteousness in our children. These are our rights and responsibilities before God.

The church also has a role to play in the process of courtship. First, pastors need to teach biblical morality and purity. I stand firm against dating in the church among teenagers. When I say I don't want any dating inside the church, I'm not telling parents that their children can't date. I am saying that the church is not the place to express that relationship. Your child can go to the mall and hang out with a girlfriend or boyfriend or spend unsupervised time alone, but those are not acceptable practices in our church. We just let teenage couples and their parents know that when they come to church, they won't be sitting together hugging as a couple.

There's much to be said about the abstinence movements within our churches today. But most of us are not blind to the reality that teens are having sex outside of marriage. And some of those teens belong to us. There is enormous pressure on our young people, from the culture and their peers, to engage in premarital sex. If a young girl has had seven boyfriends from the time she is twelve until she turns nineteen, the odds are that she will find it more difficult to stay pure. Both parents and the church need to tell our children that dating is a serious business that leads to their forming strong physical and emotional ties that they are not ready for. God has made us stewards over our marriages, yes, but He also made us stewards over our children's values regarding marriage. We are the ones who lay the foundations upon which our children will build their lives.

THE REALITY OF PREMATURE TIES

Any kind of intimate relationship carries tremendous emotional and mental strain. When a girl between the ages of twelve and seventeen finds herself in a relationship with a young boy, it is an unconfirmed marriage contract. The only emotional difference between dating and marriage is the vow and the license.

By the time young people get married, they may well have formed and broken up many relationships. They are acquainted with being cheated on and disrespected. They have given their hearts and minds to another many times and have experienced all the pain and torment of a relationship without any of the true security of marriage. Some parents do not take these experiences of "puppy love" seriously and pass them off as just another phase. But many youth are wounded for life in the context of these relationships, simply because we parents have not taken them seriously.

Healthy marriages are based upon a mutual trust and transparency that is based on a covenant relationship and commitment. This trust and transparency is something that happens only when the parties spend time and work at getting to know each other. Unfortunately, many marriages are ready for the divorce lawyers a few months after the honeymoon.

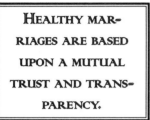

HEALTHY MAR-
RIAGES ARE BASED
UPON A MUTUAL
TRUST AND TRANS-
PARENCY.

Today couples and their families stage spectacular wedding events that prove to everyone how much they love each other. Families spend thousands of dollars on a dress, invitations, and pictures for a wedding that has only a 50 percent chance of surviving. All that money will have been spent for a wedding dress that is packed away along with pictures that nobody ever wants to see again. A year into the marriage, there is nothing to show for their investment.

There is a serious oneness that takes place between two people who are physically intimate—whether or not there has been a wedding. Any kind of intimate touching results in a joining of two people. The parties have entrusted to someone else what does not belong to him or her. Paul told us that when we become *"joined"* to another person, we are *"one flesh"* with them. (See 1 Corinthians 6:16.) Of course, he was not talking about the dating experience in this context, but any time we give ourselves to another person, we leave ourselves open to a world of pain. Trust must be earned, not given away. We would never think of allowing some young man to drive our car without knowing where he is going. Many times we give less thought to our kids than to our cars.

WHAT WE ARE SAYING

Marriage is two people deciding that they are going to build a life together. But they will have no idea what kind of life to build or how to build it unless both the church and the family accept their responsibilities to guide the process of courtship. Pastors need to take an active interest in and stop turning a deaf ear to what is certainly happening in their congregations. Parents need to get involved and stop hoping that the problem will either take care of itself or go away. This is true whether it is a first or second marriage. The principles and the problems are the same regardless of age. If someone is entering into a second marriage after the death of a spouse or after a divorce, parents may no longer be around to help. But there are older brothers and sisters in the church who can help to keep the couple accountable.

The blueprints have been drawn up and the lumber delivered. We know what we want to build. Now it's time to begin. Here are a few points to remember as we start:

- Courtship is a time of preparation, not a test drive.

- Parents have the right and responsibility to take part in their children's courtship.

- The church needs to take a stand on the dating practices of its youth.

- Courtship is serious business that affects us for life.

CHAPTER THREE

THREE BUILDING
BLOCKS

CHAPTER THREE

THREE BUILDING BLOCKS

WHAT THINGS HOLD THE HOUSE TOGETHER?

Now that we have a vision and have established a firm base upon which to build, we need to begin to put some foundation blocks in place. Over the years of building our own household, we have learned there are a few building blocks that support everything: *communication, comfort,* and *conflict resolution*. Everything we build rests on and depends on these three blocks.

The cornerstone of a sane house is *communication*. Without communication, everything else falls apart.

COMMUNICATION

Humans are unique. Of all the creatures of God, only humans have the ability and desire to let other people know what we think and feel. In fact, it was for the

| THE CORNERSTONE OF A SANE HOUSE IS COMMUNICATION. |

purpose of communication with God that we were created in the first place! Communication was open and without fear in the very beginning. There was an innocence and security in the relationships between God and man, as well as between man and man. After man went his own way, however, he began to hold back some of that openness. Still, the only way to establish trust in the house is to talk.

It is important that people living in the same house talk to one another. Communication begins and ends with a desire to know what is on the other person's heart. In our house we often ask each other, "How are you doing? Is there anything new going on that I need to know? What's going on with you?" Communication begins when *we* begin communicating. There is no better way to get others to talk to us than to ask them about themselves. The key to effective communication is openness and trust, and there is no better way to establish trust than to express care and concern for the other person.

Communication gives us a sense of security; we know that when trials and issues come along, someone is there who cares. Questions, doubts, and fears can be brought out into the light and dealt with. The people in the house with us can bring us wisdom and insight in handling difficult issues. They know us better than anyone else does.

Jeannie: It is very important for husbands to communicate with wives beyond a short response. In earlier stages of our marriage, my husband would offer short, direct answers to my concerns, but I never felt as though he heard me. I'd ask him questions, and instead of receiving direction or understanding, I'd be left up in the air trying to figure everything out on my own. I felt alone and unimportant. Women have a need for expression and understanding; otherwise they feel ignored. Even if there is no immediate or specific answer to the issues we raise, there needs to be an acknowledgment that at least we were really heard.

Another important facet of communication is the "follow-through." Once there has been a decision or an answer given, everybody must follow through with it. If you decide to spend a certain amount of money on something in the house, then do it! If you don't, then beware, because the trust that forms the basis of all communication will be destroyed. The rule, then, is that if you say it, you'd better do it. Otherwise that issue will remain unresolved and will come up again and again like a splinter in your big toe.

There is a natural order that goes on between men and women. Women can have a tendency to be a little emotional at times. (This is an official, certified understatement.) So, when the husband is talking to his wife, he must be careful not only in what he says, but also in how he says it. Husbands need to be direct and honest, yes, but they must think through what they are saying and how it is going to be received on the other end. If they don't, communication will not take place. Communication is the communion of two hearts, and it starts by considering the other heart first.

Bishop: Communication is a challenge for us men. It does not come as naturally for us as it often does for our wives. We think a grunt uttered at the proper frequency should be good enough to get our point across. If our wives disagree with us, we feel as though our integrity and manhood are being challenged. Men tend to use half the words that women do and expect twice the results. We think things out for a while and only speak when we have made up our minds. We don't include our wives or the rest of the family in our thoughts. We just utter a decision. This leaves everybody else out of the process and doesn't settle anything.

Maybe James was speaking to *us* when he said, *"Let every man be swift to hear, slow to speak, slow to wrath; for the wrath of man does not produce the righteousness of God"* (James 1:19–20). When we speak and are not understood, we get angry—we yell and holler. Then our wives get hurt and cry, and everything is out of control. James recommended a different method: Start by listening more and speaking less. And when we speak, we should have something to say that produces the righteousness of God rather than the emotion of man.

We need to choose our words a little more carefully and speak so that our wives feel safe and as though they are part of the process. Then there will be much more peace in the house.

Communication is very important if we are to keep our households in one piece. At the same time, we need to realize that there will be times of misunderstanding. We must learn to settle these things if we are to maintain good communication.

CONFLICT RESOLUTION

Jesus said that it is inevitable that stumbling blocks will come. (See Luke 17:1.) Stumbling blocks and differences of opinion will come, but they don't have to destroy us. It is not whether or not we will have conflicts, but rather how we handle them, that will determine how much peace there is in the house.

Sometimes marriage seems more like a battle than a love relationship. Contrary to what all the current humanistic sociologists say, men and women are different. They think differently and have different opinions about what is important. Where there is diversity, there will be inevitable disagreement. It's just part of the package. But if we are not careful, these differences can turn into battles that nobody wins. We cannot look at our marriages and households as gladiatorial arenas where we try to exercise power and authority. In a battle for control, nobody ever wins. If men have to force their

> IN A BATTLE FOR CONTROL, NOBODY EVER WINS.

authority on their wives, then they don't really have authority in the first place.

The best way to approach conflict is to stop trying to prove that we are right. In other words, stop trying to win. Conflict is the result of communication that has broken down. The first thing to do is to try to restore the flow of communication. Instead of firing off another insult or executing another power play, we should sit down at the table and try to bring a cease-fire. Once again, we need to stop talking and start listening. If we want someone to follow us, we need to back off and allow that person to move toward us.

After peace has been restored, we need to approach the conflict by going back to where it started. What was the last thing we agreed on? Where did things break down? It comes as a surprise to many people that there can be more than one valid opinion on some things. Sometimes gender has nothing to do with why there is disagreement in the house. People are just different. It is true that somehow opposites are attracted to one another. So why are we so surprised when we don't agree?

Sometimes our households look more like *The Odd Couple* than *The Bill Cosby Show*. Remember Felix and Oscar? Oscar was a slob, and Felix was a compulsive everything. Felix had to have everything in its place, while Oscar had no place for anything. His room was littered with dirty laundry and old tuna sandwiches or leftover pizza. Most of the conflicts between the two men were the result of one trying to change or cross over into the domain of the other. Both went crazy trying to change the other. Somehow, by the end of the show, they always put their friendship back together. Real life, however, does not run in thirty-minute episodes with everybody living happily ever after. It takes work on both parties' ends to keep the lines of trust and communication open.

We are not going to change how our spouse thinks. Instead, we should decide what is important and sit down at the table to figure out what the boundaries are. We can negotiate things like having time and space to ourselves or how often we visit the in-laws. Unless we set these boundaries in place, we will spend all of our time arguing and risk further unnecessary stress in the house. The key component is our understanding that nothing—no issue and no problem—is more important than the marriage relationship. If we are to maintain a "sane house," it will require a lot of grace.

Many times people enter into the marriage relationship with unresolved past wounds, with ungodly abuses that have been perpetrated on them. In my own case, I was raised in a household with a father who was rarely there, who left us to make our own way. So, by the time I got into marriage, my ideas about home and family needed to be adjusted to include things like compassion and commitment, which I had never seen modeled. Again, whatever wounds we carry with us into marriage will leave us less able to deal objectively with everyday marriage issues. We may be controlled by fear or low self-esteem. Our spouse may not have been raised with love and support and therefore doesn't know how to live in a normal relationship. It will take time and understanding to overcome these damaged emotions, but through patience and understanding, healing and communication can be restored.

Once again, communication is perhaps the most important building block upon which to build a sane house. Occasionally communication will break down into conflict. Many times this conflict is the result of feeling that our personal space has been invaded. Sometimes we can't feel at home in our own house. Home needs to be a place where we feel safe and able to be ourselves. Home needs to be a place of *comfort*.

COMFORT

Some time ago Jeannie and I were blessed to be able to move into a brand-new house that we built on a plot of land we had purchased. Everything in our home was clean and new. It was all white, with white chairs and white carpet with mirrors and gold curtains. It was beautiful. It looked like a house you might see in an architectural design magazine. The house was built exactly the way we wanted it, and it provided a place of comfort and rest from our growing work in ministry.

After moving into our new home, I was bent on paying it off as soon as possible. I was on the road a lot and slept in our new home only thirty-five or forty nights out of a year. The fear and instability of my childhood had made me somewhat of a workaholic.

Upon coming home one afternoon after a long ministry trip, I walked into the living room to sit down and put my feet up. Suddenly I heard a voice say, "Come outta there!" So of course I turned around and quickly left my living room. This room was a highly decorated and attractive room set aside to entertain. It was a room designed to impress guests, but it was a "no fly zone" for us. This was not a room where we could kick off our shoes and relax.

Somehow it didn't seem fair to me that others were allowed to sit in my living room, but I was not welcome. Others ate from my fine china, drank from my crystal glasses, and wiped their mouths with my cloth napkins, while we normally had to use paper plates and napkins. It dawned on me that I might die and some other man could be in my house, with his shoes off, sitting on my couch, walking on my carpet, and eating off of my life's work and success. This was my house, built by hard work, but I did not feel at home. I could not be totally comfortable in my own home.

One of the things we have learned is that when we are home, we are home; and when we are at work, we are at work. The family has to have a "sacred space" that needs to remain undisturbed. I have learned how to compartmentalize my life. I have an office upstairs in our home from which I do business. However, when I walk out the office door, I leave business behind. I don't even like to answer ministry or business calls when I am at home and out of the office. When the phone rings at our house, I don't even look at the caller ID, let alone answer it.

In fact, I'm not even really sure how to check all the machines on which people like to leave me messages.

I'm not trying to be indifferent about the needs of those who might call me, but they have homes they enjoy as well. Many times, what people consider to be "emergencies" are problems that have boiled for a long time before. Most of them will keep until the next day. If I do not respect my home space, neither will anyone else.

Ministry is ministry, and home is home. There are times when some ministry issue is not settled when we leave church, but we don't bring it in the house. We stay in the car until we finish the discussion. When we bring those ministry concerns into the house, they take up our personal space and cause some resentment in the family. If ministry crowds out our personal family space, then there is an unspoken message received by every member of the house that the family is less important than the others we minister to. Paul told Timothy that *"if anyone does not provide for his own, and especially for those of his household, he has denied the faith and is worse than an unbeliever"* (1 Timothy 5:8). We are to provide *"especially"* for those in our households. When we allow the business of ministry to push our families aside, we create wounds that some other ministry is going to have to heal. Home is home; work is work. We need to keep them separate if we are going to keep the peace.

WHAT WE ARE SAYING

All three building blocks we have discovered are necessary to building and keeping a sane and solid house. Remember, the three blocks are communication, comfort, and conflict resolution, and once more we say that communication is part of all three. Keep the lines of communication open. When communication lines get plugged, don't do anything else until they get unplugged.

Here are a few things to remember as we move on to establish a solid and sane house.

- Communication begins when we begin communicating.

- Women need to feel as though they are heard.

- We must speak in a way so as to be understood, not just heard.

- To resolve conflict, we need to stop trying to prove that we are right.

- Every family and every individual needs some sacred space.

- If we don't respect our sacred space, neither will anyone else.

PART TWO

BUILDING THE HOUSE

CHAPTER FOUR

IS THERE A MAN IN THE HOUSE?

CHAPTER FOUR

IS THERE A MAN IN THE HOUSE?

WHO PROVIDES THE FINANCIAL, PHYSICAL, AND EMOTIONAL COVERING IN YOUR HOUSE?

Then Judah took a wife for Er his firstborn, and her name was Tamar. But Er, Judah's firstborn, was wicked in the sight of the LORD, and the LORD killed him. And Judah said to Onan, "Go in to your brother's wife and marry her, and raise up an heir to your brother." But Onan knew that the heir would not be his; and it came to pass, when he went in to his brother's wife, that he emitted on the ground, lest he should give an heir to his brother. And the thing which he did displeased the LORD; therefore He killed him also. Then Judah said to Tamar his daughter-in-law, "Remain a widow

in your father's house till my son Shelah is grown." For he said, "Lest he also die as his brothers." And Tamar went and dwelt in her father's house.
—Genesis 38:6–11

Tamar sat by the side of the road outside the village of Timnath, having exchanged her mourning clothes for the garb of a temple prostitute. The veil she wore concealed her true identity in this most public of places. She who should have been safe and warm in her home was reduced to the station of a high-class hooker. How could this be, that this woman through whom the Messiah would come—a woman of great destiny—could become so degraded as to sell herself? Her shame and degradation were the result of being "uncovered"; she was left without provision or choice by men who would not accept their responsibility to cherish and protect her. She was married, yet alone—a condition all too common even in the household of God.

Many wives today find themselves "uncovered" by their husbands and so have to take things into their own hands. When I was small, my mother had to resort to desperate tactics to get us kids what we needed. My father, who left a trail of children behind him with several different women, never really provided for us. He just wasn't there, and we seldom knew where he was. My mother had three children by my father, and because he was absent, sometimes she had to resort to desperate methods to provide for us. Her desperation led her to do things totally out of her character.

Once she actually stole clothing for me because we just didn't have any money. I still get choked up today when I remember some of the things my mom had to do because she was left "uncovered" by her husband.

The biblical account of Tamar shows us how important it is that men understand their role as the *covering* for a household. To be a covering means to accept responsibility to provide for the needs of the whole person of the wife—financially, physically, and emotionally. A series of men failed to cover Tamar by ignoring their position before God and focusing on themselves. Actually, Tamar's problems started and ended with Judah.

Judah, a Jew and the son of Jacob, married a Canaanite woman out of lust and physical attraction rather than godly motivation. His was not a marriage arranged or blessed by his father or family. In fact, it was hardly a marriage at all! It was a carnal relationship based purely on physical attraction. The Bible says that Judah *"saw"* a daughter of a Canaanite and *"took her"* for himself (Genesis 38:2 KJV). From the beginning, Judah was interested only in using her for his own pleasure. He was not a covering for this Canaanite woman; rather, she became a convenience for him.

Too many men today marry because of physical attraction to a woman. They can see no farther than the honeymoon, and they fail to take the needs of their wives into account. They have not taken responsibility for the wholeness and well-being of their wives. Husbands have little or no understanding of the concept of "covering" a wife—and the culture today does nothing to help the

> THE WORLD TELLS A MAN THAT, IF HE TIRES OF HIS WIFE, HE CAN GET ANOTHER, YOUNGER MODEL.

problem. The world tells us that if things don't work out—if a man gets tired of his wife—he can just get rid of her and get another, younger model. When things get tough, they just go out and "take" another wife.

The apple didn't fall far from the tree with Judah's sons and their attitudes toward women. Judah again *"took"* a Canaanite girl for his eldest son, Er. Er, raised by a Canaanite mother, was evil before the Lord and died. Though the Bible is not specific about what kind of evil Er did, we can be sure that it was something that was aimed more at pleasing himself than God. Whatever it was, God had to destroy Er. What else would we expect? In Jacob's prophecy over Judah, he made it clear that the Messiah would be born through Judah's sons, saying, *"The scepter shall not depart from Judah, nor a lawgiver from between his feet, until Shiloh* [Jesus the Messiah] *comes; and to Him shall be the obedience of the people"* (Genesis 49:10). God would not allow the Messiah to come through the loins of an unrepentant pagan who worshipped false gods.

Then it was the second brother's turn. The legal custom was that if a brother died and left a wife, the next brother was to take her as a wife and to raise children to preserve the name and inheritance of the dead brother. But in typical selfish fashion, this younger brother, Onan, spilled his seed on the ground, thereby depriving Tamar of children and an inheritance. He sought pleasure without purpose. God was displeased with Onan's selfishness, and another brother died and left Tamar uncovered. Neither son took his place as a covering for Tamar.

Now comes Judah. Remember that Tamar was the wife of his own son. She was taken from the household of her father and placed in the household of Judah's son. She became the responsibility of Judah's household. She left her family behind and placed herself at the mercy and under the covering of a man from God's own people—an heir to the promises of God! It was clearly Judah's responsibility to provide for his daughter-in-law, but instead he told her to put on mourning clothes and go back to her father's house from where he had taken her. (See Genesis 38:11.) Since women were not allowed to work or even to beg, Judah was telling her to go and live off of the scraps from her father's table—to live off the charity of others. Once again Tamar was *uncovered*. What could she do but to provide her own covering? She felt as if she was left with no choice but to resort to desperate and uncharacteristic measures to get what was rightfully hers.

While Tamar sat in mourning clothes, she heard that her father-in-law was going to be in the neighborhood, in the village of Timnath. Hearing this, her desperate mind conceived a plan. If a husband would not cover her, she would "cover herself" in the clothes of a temple prostitute. (See Genesis 38:14.) The name of the place where she would meet Judah, Timnath, could be interpreted as the place of allotment or inheritance. Since Judah had deprived Tamar of her rightful inheritance and position, she would go about getting what was rightfully hers in another way.

Along came Judah. He was no different here from when he *"saw"* and took a Canaanite woman for his own pleasure. Once again, Judah *"saw"* the opportunity for pleasure in the veil of a prostitute and lusted after her. (See Genesis 38:15.) Tamar's veil concealed her true identity, and Judah did not recognize her. So Judah negotiated a price for his pleasure and had sexual relations with Tamar, his own daughter-in-law. This was considered to be incest by God and a sin worthy of death. (See Leviticus 20:12.) As a guarantee of his intention to pay her the price that he promised, Judah gave her his seal, his cord, and his staff. These would be a pledge that he would send the price they had agreed upon. The seal, cord, and staff, however, were the very symbols of his identity and authority. So desperate and selfish was Judah that he left these in the hands of someone he believed to be a prostitute.

Tamar then found herself pregnant by her own father-in-law. When Judah learned that Tamar, his son's wife, was pregnant, he sought "justice." Eventually he learned the truth that *he* was the father of her unborn child and, in fact, worthy of death. Faced with the obvious truth that he had been less than righteous toward his daughter-in-law, Judah at last took her into his care. She would at last be "covered" as she should have been from the time she was taken as a wife.

Just as every area of a house has a purpose and an identity, just as each room has a specific function, so each partner in a marriage has a function and a purpose to fulfill according to design. Let's focus more on the "covering" role and the role of the man in the house.

The Role of the Man in the House

The man is to be the covering presence in the home. The apostle Paul referred to the role of the husband as *"head"* of the household.

> *But I want you to know that the head of every man is Christ, the head of woman is man, and the head of Christ is God.* (1 Corinthians 11:3)

> *Wives, submit to your own husbands, as to the Lord. For the husband is head of the wife, as also Christ is head of the church; and He is the Savior of the body.* (Ephesians 5:22–23)

> *Wives, submit to your own husbands, as is fitting in the Lord.* (Colossians 3:18)

Being the *"head"* means that the man has been given a place of responsibility and accountability. He is, in effect, like a managing partner in the marriage. This doesn't mean that he rules over the house as a dictator; rather, he has a responsibility to put things in order in the house. The husband is sort of the managing partner, but he is still an *equal* partner in the marriage. The peace

> THE HUSBAND IS THE MANAGING PARTNER, BUT HE IS STILL AN EQUAL PARTNER.

and stability of the home depend on the condition of his partnership with his wife. If she feels smothered or uncovered, she may have to resort to manipulation to get what she needs. She must be an equal partner with an equal say in the house, with the husband accepting leadership in final decisions. God has delegated authority to the husband and made him accountable to the Head of all things, who is Jesus Christ.

Within the authority of the husband's position is the obligation to lay down his life for his wife and family just as Jesus laid down His life for His own bride. To lay down his life means that the husband puts his needs *after* those of his wife. The source of this authority flows from the covenant he enters in marriage. The man makes the vow to provide for and take care of his wife. This covenant is unconditional; it does not go away when troubles come along or when the wife goes from size 2 to size 22!

Jeannie: When we first married, I was a size zero! Needless to say, I am no longer, but my husband's love and commitment to me has only gotten stronger. He has laid his life down for me many times. He's laid it down when I've had a bad day. He's laid it down when he has had a bad day. Because of the way he exercises his authority, I love and respect him more. Because he has honored me, I find it easy to honor him.

MONEY CAN'T BUY YOU LOVE

It is true, as the old song says, that money can't buy you love. Because some men have not seen good role models or been taught what it means to be a godly and responsible husband, they have no idea what it takes to hold a family together. "What do you want?" men often growl when spending money on the kids, because that's their method of managing the house. It is not enough to buy sneakers and Snickers for the kids without providing the emotional and mental support needed for a healthy household.

Bishop: My dad was never around, and this can be the case for many men. I had to learn, by the grace of God, what it means to be a husband and a father. I have learned that being the managing partner of a household takes a lot of work and a lot of dying to myself. It wasn't something I could buy my way into or out of.

There is a need today for mentors in the body of Christ to teach men how to be covering husbands. There is a story from Africa of a place where several young male elephants went on a rampage of destruction with frequent and deadly conflicts between them. Seeing this, the game wardens transported a few older male elephants to the neighborhood. The younger males soon began to gather around the old bulls and, within a short while, the youngsters were calmed. The problem was that the young males had no role models to demonstrate responsibility to the herd. They needed mentors. So do husbands. Many of the problems we see today with gangs and drugs are the direct result of uncovered households. The body of Christ has the potential to bring restoration to our culture by encouraging husbands to become the covering presence that the Lord has called them to be.

The final result of Tamar's covering being restored by Judah was that she brought forth twin sons. (See Genesis 38:27–30.) These sons were mentioned, along with Tamar, in the genealogy of Jesus Christ, the King of Kings. (See Matthew 1:1–16.) A household covered by a godly husband will bring forth the fragrance of Christ, the ultimate covering Bridegroom.

WHAT WE ARE SAYING

Here are a few things we have learned about the role of the husband:

- Husbands are to provide physical, financial, and emotional stability for the house.

- Husbands are to be managing but equal partners in the house.

- Husbands are to provide headship, not a dictatorship.

- Husbands who don't cover wives force those wives to cover themselves.

- Husbands who honor their wives will themselves be honored.

CHAPTER FIVE

COVERED, NOT CONCEALED

Covered, Not Concealed

What does it mean to be in submission?

Wives, submit to your own husbands, as to the Lord. For the husband is head of the wife, as also Christ is head of the church; and He is the Savior of the body. Therefore, just as the church is subject to Christ, so let the wives be to their own husbands in everything.
—Ephesians 5:22–24

There is that word again—*submission.* It's a word that makes some women angry and some husbands arrogant. Submission seems like a win for men and a loss for women, where all the eggs are placed in the husband's basket—a one-sided deal dreamed up by some guy who didn't like or trust women. Unfortunately, if we believe this, we have missed God's point regarding submission and the role of women within the marriage relationship. Remember, to build a sane house and a solid marriage, it takes two equal and responsible partners.

The husband's position before God is to provide a covering for the household that leads to physical, financial, and emotional wholeness. However, there is a difference between covering and smothering. Wives are to be covered, not concealed by the husband. Wives have a unique role within the marriage under the covering of a godly husband. They are still individuals with unique gifts and abilities. It is important to realize that wives do not cease to be individuals when they say "I do." As in any other relationship, each party brings strengths and weaknesses into the marriage. God, however, laminates those strengths and weaknesses together within the marriage to make one new strong person. *"Therefore shall a man leave his father and his mother, and shall cleave unto his wife: and they shall be one flesh"* (Genesis 2:24).

"SUB-MISSION"

Paul told us that wives need to be *"subject to,"* or in *submission* to their own husbands. Some men might use this Scripture to rule over their wives, but Paul was telling us just the opposite. He said that women are to submit to *"their own husbands,"* not to all men.

Submission has nothing to do with gender; it has to do with order in an equal partnership. Women are not to be subject to all men, only to *"their own husbands."*

Wives are called to be in *sub*-mission to their husbands. *Sub* means to be under or in order. It doesn't say anything about value—only order. To be in sub-mission, then, means that the wife is in order under the same mission. The mission of the marriage is to bring glory to Christ. When

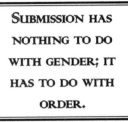

SUBMISSION HAS NOTHING TO DO WITH GENDER; IT HAS TO DO WITH ORDER.

the Bible says *submit,* some hear the word *doormat.* Although some husbands may believe that because they are the head, the wife must be the tail, this is not what it means for the wife to be in submission. The Bible was not written to force wives to take orders or to "keep women in line." Some men use the Scriptures to dominate their wives or even coerce them to have sex. But the Word is clear. What we are called to is an equal partnership in which both parties have specific roles. Submission is not submersion or slavery.

A wife's ability to be in submission to her husband is a result of trust. Submission is not automatic; it is the decision of the wife to honor her husband and support him as head of the house. To do this she must trust that her husband loves and respects her. It is easy for a wife to be in submission to a husband who has taken his place as the head or managing partner of the household to provide for and protect his family. It's easy to submit to a husband who lays down his own life as Christ laid down His for His bride. Trust is the covering under which the wife will be able to submit to her husband.

A husband who is secure in his place as the head of the house will not try to conceal or keep his wife "in her place." On the contrary, he will do whatever he can to help her be all that she can be—he will help her to express her unique gifts and abilities. Such is the role and responsibility of the "covering husband."

Some time ago I asked my wife, "What do you want to do with your life?" I encouraged her to set goals and to pursue them. She has many gifts, and it is up to me to encourage her to develop them. A few weeks later, she came to me and said, "I want to go back to school." I was pleased with her decision. Now my wife has an accounting business in which she handles millions of dollars, manages properties, makes sure the bills are paid on time, does payroll, pays insurance, and all kinds of things. It is not enough for me just to acknowledge Jeannie; I must invest in her life. I feel free to invest in her because I feel secure in my own position before God. I have reaped the benefits of my investment countless times.

Jeannie: A wife who is covered and not concealed by her husband must also take responsibility to develop her gifts and abilities. It's not about just looking good, having your hair and nails done, or going out with girlfriends. We must learn to understand the business portion of the household. In the early part of our marriage, I didn't know much about running the household. My husband took care of everything. I didn't know how to pay the bills or how to balance checkbooks. If something would have had happened to my husband during that time, it would have meant catastrophe for me and my children. I would have been left with two girls, a house I could not pay for, and bills for which I had no address to mail the check.

At a young age, I left a home in which my father took care of everything. He paid all the bills and handled all the business for the house without involving my mother. So I grew up not knowing where the water or electric company were and, what was worse, I was afraid to go to any of those places because it was all such a mystery to me. I was raised by a mother who was in the same situation—she was not an equal partner in the house. So I went into marriage totally unprepared and dependant upon my husband to take care of everything from paying the bills to shopping for groceries. It's important to know the business part of the house. It's equally important for the husbands talk to their wives about what's going on—the insurance policies in the home, maintaining the the household, and so on. Wives must be equal partners in all facets of the household.

A sane and peaceful house is possible only when both partners are in place doing what the Lord has enabled them to do in every realm.

Two Heads Are Never Better than One

Bishop: There cannot be two heads in a household. Anything that has two heads is a freak destined for the circus. We cannot go in two directions at the same time. Someone has to determine which way to go. If

> THERE CANNOT BE
> TWO HEADS IN A
> HOUSEHOLD.

a husband and wife are driving in the car and come to a fork in the road, they can go only one way. The husband may be driving the car, but he is not going to just grab the steering wheel and go where he wants to go; he will ask the wife which way she thinks they should go. Many times, because of the responsibilities in the house, the wife may be the one to determine which way they have to go, whether to the grocery store or to the doctor's office. Both have a stake in the final destination because they are both in the car. The husband cannot go without his wife, and the wife cannot go without her husband. Wherever we go, we are going together.

Sometimes a husband does not lead as the spiritual head of the house. He may provide for the family in natural concerns, but he doesn't become the priest that he needs to be for the home. However, there are not two heads in the house, one natural and the other spiritual. There is still only one head! It does not work when the wife tries to fill in the void. She does not have the grace to fulfill the husband's role. So what is she to do when the husband does not take his place as the spiritual head of the family? Peter gave the answer.

> *Wives, likewise, be submissive to your own husbands, that even if some do not obey the word, they, without a word, may be won by the conduct of their wives, when they observe your chaste*

conduct accompanied by fear. Do not let your adornment be merely outward; arranging the hair, wearing gold, or putting on fine apparel; rather let it be the hidden person of the heart, with the incorruptible beauty of a gentle and quiet spirit, which is very precious in the sight of God. (1 Peter 3:1–4)

Many marriages are ripped apart because a wife tries to cover the spiritual bases. Regardless of whether or not the husband takes his place as the spiritual head, he is *still* the spiritual head and must be treated as such. But how can a wife see a husband as the spiritual head when he has no relationship with the Lord? A better question is, how will he ever take his place as the head if the wife doesn't start treating him as such?

We have heard frustrated and tearful wives say, "My husband is just not ever going to be the spiritual head of our house. He just doesn't have the same kind of relationship with the Lord that I have." I'm sure that Pastor Simon Peter dealt with the same complaint from the wives in his congregation. His advice to frustrated wives was that they needed to demonstrate 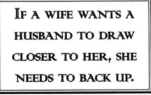 a *"gentle and quiet spirit."* It is a fact that if a wife wants a husband to draw closer to her, she needs to back up. Name one wife who has hounded her husband into heaven. If we want to draw someone, we need to back up and allow that person to move toward us. Just back up!

The quiet and gentle spirit that a wife displays comes from her trust in God. She will be quiet only when she believes that the Lord has things in hand. She can be gentle only if she senses the power of God around her. It is God through the Holy Spirit who draws all men to Himself. Jesus said, *"No one can come to Me unless the Father who sent Me draws him"* (John 6:44). Salvation is God's business; faith is our business. Live a life that is *"precious in the sight of God"* (1 Peter 1:4), and the Holy Spirit will draw a husband into his position. How else will a husband know to lead if the wife will not follow?

The Bible gives us a great example of a wife who was both in and out of submission to her husband: Sarah.

> *For in this manner, in former times, the holy women who trusted in God also adorned themselves, being submissive to their own husbands, as Sarah obeyed Abraham, calling him lord, whose daughters you are if you do good and are not afraid with any terror.* (1 Peter 3:5–6)

Sarah was a wife in submission to her husband, Abraham. Peter used her as the example of a *"holy"* woman who obeyed Abraham. She called him *"lord,"* which is to say that she placed her total trust in him to follow God and provide for her. Sarah's name in Hebrew means "princess." A princess is not a slave or inferior in any way. A princess is one who shares the reign from the throne.

The role of the wife in the household is one of sharing in all the important matters of the house from an important position. To be in submission is to be submitted to the same mission as the husband. It is not to be in a place where the wife is *"afraid with any terror."* It is to be a place of trust and security in the order of God.

If we are to release the grace and power of God to build a sane house, both husband and wife must be in place. Paul told wives to be in submission to their own husbands *"as is fitting in the Lord"* (Colossians 3:18). Each partner has a role to "fit" into, and each has an equal responsibility to support the other in his or her role. It is also true that both partners will occasionally blow it and step out of their roles. Even Sarah, the role model of a submitted and co-reigning wife, stepped out from under her husband's covering—and the incident resulted in Ishmael. It is grace, not perfection, that holds partners together. Grace covers us when we uncover ourselves.

The role of the wife is important and critical in building strong, godly houses. It is a role that depends on trusting in God. Sarah was one who *"trusted in God"* (1 Peter 3:5) and submitted to her husband. It is only in trusting God that both husband and wife are able to fulfill their respective roles and responsibilities. When *"husbands...dwell with...understanding, giving honor to the wife,"* and wives find security in their positions, then both are *"heirs together of the grace of life,"* bringing glory to God (v. 7).

WHAT WE ARE SAYING

Here are a few things we have learned about the role of the wife:

- Sub-mission means that the wife is in order and on the same mission as her husband.

- Submission is not submersion or slavery.

- The ability of the wife to be in submission is grounded in trust.

- There are not two heads of a household, one natural and one spiritual.

- A husband will not act like the spiritual head until the wife treats him as such.

- Husbands need to invest in the gifts and abilities of their wives.

- Grace covers us in our roles when we uncover ourselves.

CHAPTER SIX

WHEN FOUNDATIONS SETTLE

CHAPTER SIX

WHEN FOUNDATIONS SETTLE

ARE THERE SIGHS AND GROANS IN YOUR HOUSE?

As we mentioned earlier, we recently moved into a new house. After we were all moved and settled into our new home, we occasionally heard a slight creaking kind of sound, which seemed to come from beneath the house somewhere. No, it wasn't poltergeists; it was just the sound of a new house settling on its foundation. Things aren't always quite settled in a brand-new home. As people move in with their furniture and belongings, new stresses are added to the foundation and the main support beams, but it's not necessarily serious. This settling process may take a while—maybe even several years—to run its course. It is inevitable that the creaks and groans of settlement will be heard to some degree in any new house, but if the foundation is solid, it will not crack.

We have learned that there is "settling" that takes place in new households similar to what happens in a new house. Despite our best efforts and careful preparation, new stresses like children, money problems, and the everyday realities of life will cause shifting and settling on the foundations of our households. There will be the creaks and groans of settling, but the foundation will not crack so long as the foundation remains strong and solid. What stresses can settle on a marriage? We're going to focus on a few that we have encountered in the settling of our own household. Perhaps you already have a list of things that "go bump" in the middle of a marriage as well!

THE CREAKING SOUNDS OF REALITY

Think for a moment…who are you? What is important to you? What takes up the space of your heart? What makes you angry, joyful, or afraid? Chances are that you can't answer all of these questions. The fact is that most of the answers change with maturity. Things that were important when we were five or fifteen may not be the same things that are important when we're fifty. We will develop different tastes in food, music, and even people as we grow—and

> THE FIRST THING THAT CHANGES AFTER MARRIAGE IS OUR UNDERSTANDING OF OURSELVES.

there is no greater influence for change than marriage. Usually, the first thing that changes after marriage is our understanding of ourselves.

Many new marriage relationships end up in trouble because both individuals are still developing while simultaneously giving themselves to the other person. You see, marriage is a sculpting experience—it's like placing our lives and personalities in the hands of another individual and inviting him or her to mold and reshape us. When we search for a mate, we see everything in terms of what we think is ideal. Needless to say, those ideals are usually unrealistic and change greatly with time. When both individuals get involved in the relationship, they find out that what they thought was their ideal mate isn't so ideal after all. So the first casualty of our idealistic expectations is *us*.

Marriage requires a lot of stepping aside and compromising, a lot of thinking about someone besides ourselves. The first time the husband wants to lie around on a Sunday afternoon and watch football while the wife needs a little personal attention, reality will set in. When a man sees his ideal princess with her face covered in some kind of beauty mud, those bluebirds of happiness are going to have to clear their throats to sing. As reality sets in and we live a little while with our spouses, we find out that we are a little less selfless, a little less spiritual than we first believed. We find ourselves saying things we never thought we would say. With each pair of panty hose hung over the shower and with every thoughtless remark about burned beans will come a remolding of personality and a deeper revelation of who we are.

I was married eight or nine years before I rediscovered who I really was. Keep in mind that I was a traveling evangelist who stepped onto different platforms every few days. I spoke into the lives of others and then left the pastoral work to someone else. There was no need to counsel anyone, to engage in conversations, or anything like that. It was a hit-and-run ministry. I was able to speak and live pretty much the way I wanted to and just move on. There was not much pressure to change, grow, or consider the effects of my words. Since I was away from home much of the time, I just transferred that same approach to life at home. I could simply say what I wanted to say and move on, leaving Jeannie behind in my wake.

In time, the Lord called us into pastoral ministry. I was not prepared for the changes that this new life would make in me. Pastoral ministry was quite different from evangelism. I learned that people's hearts change a little at a time, requiring patience. I learned that I was probably not as sensitive or understanding as I thought. Now when I spoke, I was the one responsible to care for the people. The same challenges and changes that began to happen in my ministry were paralleled at home. I was now at home more, and I grew sensitive in what I said and how I said it. For one thing, I developed a whole new appreciation for Jeannie and all that she had done over the years in our household.

Jeannie: It's possible for a woman to be married for several years and not know who she is. She may have lived in her parents' home to the very threshold of adulthood, when she is just discovering who she really is, then throw herself into the remolding process of marriage. Then, just when things seem to be settling down nicely, she finds out that she is pregnant and spends nine months on a continuous roller coaster of hormones and emotions. And when she gets off the ride, she still has no idea who she is.

More than anything else, women need to feel safe and secure. This is not a sociological statement; it's just a biological fact! The time that a wife needs the most attention and reassurance is at the very beginning of the marriage, just when the husband is off trying to establish his business or job and is less available. He is trying to make things go while the wife is trying to make things settle. Both actions are the result of the way God has made us.

We have come to the conclusion that who we are, or who we think our spouse is, will change dramatically throughout the course of marriage. We find that as we give ourselves to each other, we become better people than the ones we were at first, and that the one we married is more of a treasure than we had ever known. It is on the sculptor's table of marriage that the lump of unknown clay we were is transformed and molded into the masterpiece God intended.

THE CREAKING SOUNDS OF LITTLE FOOTSTEPS

Bishop: Just when we are getting over the creaking sounds of reality—just when we have begun to get comfortable with our spouse and find our role within the marriage—another little creak comes along: children.

Contrary to what many believe, a man is emotionally and physcially aware of the pregnancy experience, from conception all the way to childbirth. In a way, one could say that men *do* get pregnant! No, they don't get big bellies and crave strange foods, but men experience pregnancy along with the women and ride along on the emotional roller coasters. They may not talk about it, but they go through it.

> CONTRARY TO WHAT MANY BELIEVE, MEN *DO* GO THROUGH THE PROCESS OF PREGNANCY.

Many marriages suffer great damage during pregnancy. The glory and giddiness of the pregnancy fades very quickly into backaches and worry over future concerns of children. The couple is happy and excited for a few days, but then they begin to ask, "What are we gonna do? We have a baby coming. We need more room; we don't have enough money." The reality is that the baby will increase the expenditures of the household only slightly, so we shouldn't allow fear to overwhelm us and jeopardize the stability of our household.

When we think of having a baby, we think of college and all the future expenses. So you see, it's not the baby that wrecks the marriage; it's the frustration and unnecessary worry about the future! Parents go out and buy "stuff" and upset their household economy. Television and magazines give us a whole new level of expectations to live up to, and you get hooked into expenditures you never even thought about before you got married. You buy everything from bassinets to savings bonds and try to live up to worldly expectations.

There is sometimes a feeling of alienation between the husband and wife because of the new element that the baby introduces. Women draw closer to this child, whether the baby is still in the making or already delivered. The man may feel a little isolated because there is no way he can be as close as the mother is to the unborn baby. Now there are two institutions under 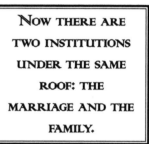 the same roof: the marriage and the family. Both are separate entities. The mistake, however, that many parents make is allowing the children to sever the marriage relationship.

This little newcomer in the mother's womb can cause severe shifting in the foundations of a marriage. The cradle isn't the only thing rocking when the baby takes its place in the order of the house. Babies can and do disrupt intimacy between parents. Every child must understand from age three or four that when a particular door in the house is closed, no one is to enter or knock at the door. We must not be deceived into thinking that children are oblivious to the intimate aspects of marriage. When children arrive, there's a strain on intimacy, whether with the sexual aspects or the personal communication that needs to happen between husband and wife.

There needs to be a clear message to children that the marriage relationship and intimacy are to be respected. Children who grow up in a home where parents are free to express intimacy tend to have a healthy expectation of being shown and giving affection. If your little girl grows up seeing her daddy hugging and kissing her mommy, then she will expect the same. The children may groan and harrumph in disgust during their adolescent years when parents hug each other, but somewhere deep inside there is a sense of great warmth and security.

We also should note that the little bundles we bring home with such joy and anticipation can become master manipulators. Kids will try every kind of psychological warfare they can think up to get what they want, and they will usually pit one parent against the other. You've heard the conversation...

"Mommy, can I go out to Tommy and Susan's house?"

"Well, go ask your father."

"Dad, can I go to Tommy and Susan's house?"

"Well, ask your mom."

"Mom said I can go as long as it's all right with you."

Meanwhile, Dad has no idea what Mom said and Mom has no idea what Dad said. Understand that no child wants Mom and Dad ripped apart forever. Children only want to separate their parents long enough to get what they want—but they will separate us if we allow them to, so don't allow it!

What have Jeannie and I learned from this? We have learned that communication and unity are the keys to sanity. Don't have those third party "remote control" conversations. If all parties are not in the room or on the telephone at the same time, don't make a decision. Nothing is so important that it requires a decision "right now." Kids, and especially teens, will use half-truths to push the limits of the law in the house. If we are not careful, our children will have us arguing over whose fault it was that the children were allowed to go to or do whatever it was they maneuvered us into. Meanwhile, the children will be in the next room mapping out their next strategy to have their way.

To stop the manipulation and mixed signals in our home, my wife and I come together at the end of every month and discuss certain things. Sound like a business? It is. We discuss things as though we are two shareholders discussing their investments. And, of course, that is exactly who we are. We each have a share in both the marriage and the family. Many couples don't know what is going on in their own homes because they don't set aside time to sit down and go over the business of house and kids. The meetings we have are held with the understanding that our children are gifts of God, and we are responsible for them. Everything can be worked out and every strategy uncovered if the husband and wife remember to be in unity and communicate on a regular basis.

Sometimes Mom and Dad will disagree on an issue, but they can never allow that disagreement to cross over and affect their marriage. Marriage is sacred, and God says, "Let no one—not your children, your mother, your grandmother, your cousin, your pastor, your bishop, no one—put it asunder. Let no one come between that union. Period!" (See Matthew 19:6, paraphrased and expanded by personal experience.)

There will be the sounds of creaking, settling foundations as long as there are children in the house. You can depend upon it. Ultimately, as we learn to keep the marriage united in order to raise the family in sanity, both institutions will withstand the occasional tremors that come our way. But there are other streams of stress that flow into our homes—other strong winds and storms that threaten to blow our houses down.

THE CREAKING SOUNDS OF STRONG WINDS AND STORMS

God uses problems and struggles that we encounter to make us stronger. Until now we have dealt mainly with destabilizing influences that arise from inside the walls of our homes. But there are a few strong gusts that challenge the integrity of our houses from the outside as well. There are the winds of financial problems, the storms of family influence and tradition, and the forces of worldly opinion that rail against the very sanctity of marriage and family.

FINANCIAL WHOAS

No, we didn't misspell *woe*; we meant *whoa*. We call them "financial whoas" because when we have problems with money, everything comes to a halt. There are few things that can tear down a house faster or more completely than financial stress. Everything can be going along great; there can be a sense of well-being and closeness between spouses and children—and then there is a call from the bank that your account has been overdrawn. Or maybe you are standing at the checkout counter at Wal-Mart and your credit card is declined. Suddenly there are storm clouds everywhere, with the deadly lightning of accusation flashing from husband to wife or wife to husband. When the checkbook doesn't balance, the foundations become like gelatin. Obviously, we could write a book just on the financial strategies for marriage. For now, however, we simply will make a few observations.

First of all, checks bounce and credit cards are declined when someone isn't keeping track of the money. These things happen by design; "we plan to fail when we fail to plan." There needs to be someone who keeps track of the money and pays the bills. Such things don't go away just because we ignore them. It is so easy to get buried in debt today with every bank on the planet sending us new credit cards. It takes only a few months to get buried under a load of debt and stress that can suffocate a marriage.

The husband might not be the one who actually sits down to pay the bills and balance the checkbook. One

spouse is probably going to be gifted and more orga-
nized than the other in this matter, but both parties
need to know what is happening with the finances
at all times so that those surprises at Wal-Mart never
happen. When both people in the marriage know what
is happening, financial challenges can be dealt with and
conquered together. When neither party knows what's
happening and those bombs come crashing through the
roof, everything else comes to a halt—*whoa!* Most of the
financial challenges can be met and dealt with as both
husband and wife stay involved. Jeannie and I make
financial concerns part of our monthly business meet-
ing. There are few, if any, surprises.

FAMILY TIES AND TRADITIONS

A good definition of tradition is "the way we always
did it." From how you stuff a turkey at Thanksgiving to
how you hang the towels in the bathroom, tradition is
a powerful influence over how families live. Traditions
themselves do not cause problems in a household; it's
the clash of a husband's traditions and the wife's traditions that makes for potential quakes in the household.
The traditions we hold and the rituals of our families
just seem normal to us. When our spouse wants to do
something a different way, it's just not normal.

Traditions are more of a problem at the beginning
of a marriage than later on. We just assume that our
spouse will see the light and do things the way we
always did them at home. However, the only assumption that we can really make is that nothing will be
the way it was when you were growing up. You create

new traditions along the way so that your children can fight over them in their own marriages. Remember that most things are negotiable and that nobody will ever make stuffing like your mother. The rest will take care of itself.

> REMEMBER THAT MOST THINGS ARE NEGOTIABLE AND THAT NOBODY WILL EVER MAKE STUFFING LIKE YOUR MOTHER DOES.

Another unsettling area is the ties that remain with our parents and family. Remember, we cannot bring them into the marriage relationship. The Bible says that we will "leave" our father and our mother and be joined to our spouses. (See Matthew 19:5.) We all nod our heads in agreement until our husband yells at us or our wife doesn't have dinner ready when we get home. Daughters often pick up the phone and call mothers, and whose side do you think Mom is going to take?

Parents can be a source of wisdom, but they ought not be confidants. We must keep matters that concern the marriage within the marriage. Don't expose personal marital things to your family. It creates bad blood between in-laws and spouses and destroys the trust that holds the marriage together. Keep those things between spouses, and, if need be, talk to an objective couple who will hear both sides of the issue. That way everybody can be heard and the foundations can remain solid.

We need to set boundaries for family. Don't be surprised when your spouse is upset because someone from your side of the family is at your house all the time. A wife doesn't want a mother-in-law telling her how to raise children or make a home. Think about it. Things are a lot different for you than they were for your parents. Many women work outside the home today in addition to raising children. Your mom is not going to understand why you have to use the microwave so often.

When we have our family in our home too much, our spouses feel "ganged up on." It's a good idea for both husband and wife to agree on who comes to the home and when. Family cannot rock the foundations if we don't give them the chance. Just remember that you will never be good enough for their son or daughter and that you are blessed to have their child as your spouse.

The foundations of our homes will creak and groan in all the ways we mentioned and many more, but they need not crumble. With each new sigh will come a deeper knowledge of who you really are and who you will become. The good thing about a house settling on its foundation is that as time goes on, it shakes less and becomes more solid. Such was and is the case with our house, and it will be in yours as well.

WHAT WE ARE SAYING

Here again are some things we have learned about settling foundations.

- The first thing that changes in our marriages is our understanding of ourselves.
- Marriage is a molding and shaping into who we really are.

- There must be a respect of the marriage relationship within the family.

- Children don't cause marital problems; worry about children does.

- You will never be good enough for your mate in his or her parents' eyes.

- Nobody will ever make stuffing like your mother does.

PART THREE

POWER IN THE HOUSE

CHAPTER SEVEN

THE BATTLE FOR CONTROL

CHAPTER SEVEN

THE BATTLE FOR

CONTROL

ARE YOU TRYING TO MANAGE OR MINISTER IN
YOUR HOME?

There is a symbol of power in most American homes today that has the potential to impact the flow of information and the well-being of everybody in the house. It is an item over which the family struggles on a continuous basis. Kids fight with kids over it; parents fight with kids and with each other over this scepter. It is passed from hand to hand, yet always seems to be misplaced. When others have it we groan and complain, but when we have it we feel empowered.

Whoever wields it determines the level of peace and happiness in the home. You guessed it—this baton of power is the TV remote control.

That's a silly example of a battle that goes on for the control of a piece of electronic equipment, but there is another battle for control taking place inside even the most solid of Christian homes that's not so funny. It is a battle in which all the players employ different kinds of tactics and strategies to gain any advantage they can. Husbands, wives, and children—even those who are otherwise in order—still try to wiggle and wedge a little advantage from time to time. The problem is that even when we know the truth and where we fit in the order of the house, we are still subject to the influences of our old sinful natures. But it does not have to remain that way. We are no longer obligated to the flesh, to the tactics of controlling one another. (See Romans 8:12.)

We have learned from experience that the only way to end this battle is to understand what is happening and to replace tactics with trust and strategies with mutual submission. Once we have an understanding of what is going on, we can stop it.

WHAT IS GOING ON?

Jeannie: In my husband's book, *Witchcraft in the Pews*, he describes a battle for control and influence that is going on in the church. He describes it in three words: *intimidation, manipulation,* and *domination.* Manipulation means, "I will trick you into doing what I want you to do." Intimidation means, "I will scare you into doing what I want you to do." And domination means, "I will make you do what I want you to do." *Witchcraft* seems like a strong word to describe what is going on in the family, but witchcraft is simply any attempt to manage or influence what other people think or do by some ungodly means. That is what is happening in most households, whether we call it that or not. There is a lot of tricking, scaring, and forcing of others to do what we want them to do.

All the ways we use to try to influence or manage people to conform to our own ways of thinking are, in effect, abuse. To abuse is to *ab*normally *use* another person. We are trying to move that person out of his or her position somehow. Manipulation is emotional abuse; intimidation is mental or physical abuse; and domination is positional abuse. We try to trick someone into feeling something, or scare him into thinking something, or push her into giving something. Regardless of the particular tactic we use to influence, we always cut the person off and deny him his full personhood.

> ALL OUR ATTEMPTS TO INFLUENCE OR MANAGE PEOPLE TO CONFORM TO OUR OWN WAYS ARE, IN EFFECT, ABUSE.

Let's take some time to see how we use each one of these strategies in the home. Once we understand what we are doing, we can choose to stop it.

MANIPULATION

When we talk about manipulation, we are referring to any attempt to manage what someone else thinks or

99

feels. In other words, we try to cause someone in the house to respond in a certain way that will benefit us. An example of this is a teenage child telling the parents that that she simply must have a certain kind of shoe or go to a particular concert because "everyone else is doing it." The teen is trying to make the parents feel either stupid or guilty for not allowing her to do what "everyone else" is doing. Sometimes it works and sometimes it doesn't, but it is clearly an attempt to manipulate parents.

One of the most popular strategies for manipulation is the "silent treatment." It is an attempt by one spouse to draw the other toward him or her by pulling away or withdrawing from the other. Ironically, the silent treatment is the very worst tactic we can use to deal with conflict. When we are trying to communicate and resolve issues and our spouse pulls further away or even walks out, it closes down all communication and leaves the other in an unsettled torment. One person is trying to communicate, and the other is trying to win.

Bishop: In the early years of our marriage, I would just shut down and stop communicating with my wife. I was *right*—I was the *man* of the house! The problem with this was that Jeannie had no way to process or express her opinion, so she just became angry and bitter. She was the one doing all the yelling, but communication is a two-way street. I was manipulating her by silent smugness. I would stand by and give her this look that said, "What are you arguing about?" I was trying to make her feel guilty and stupid for not seeing things my way. The effect of this tactic was just as offensive as knocking her to the other side of the room with a fist.

When we try to manipulate by shutting down, the result is always going to be bitterness. Women, particularly Christian women, are attacked in this way and so die inside. Hebrews tells us that we are to go after peace and settle the disagreements between us. This includes those disagreements in our houses.

> *Pursue peace with all people, and holiness, without which no one will see the Lord: looking carefully lest anyone fall short of the grace of God; lest any root of bitterness springing up cause trouble, and by this many become defiled.*
> (Hebrews 12:14–15)

When we shut down, we deny the value of the other person and cut off the grace that should be extended to our spouses. When we cut them off and devalue them, anger seethes deep inside of them and becomes bitterness. When bitterness takes root in a heart, it brings forth nothing but pain and death. Many women who have been cut off in this way are unable to give or receive love; thus they either get divorced or live in misery with manipulating and controlling husbands. Bitterness killed my mother-in-law. She developed stress, which led to high blood pressure, which led to heart problems and eventually to death. All of this happened because someone would just shut down, leaving the anger and pain inside her—where it could do the most damage.

Manipulation is not the weapon of men only, however; it also is used by women. Women may not see it as such, but sometimes they come down with a "headache" to try to convince their men to comply. This is as ungodly as any other form of manipulation because it is an attempt to control by depriving the man of intimacy. It is exactly the opposite of what is needed. Where there should be closeness and intimacy, there is only separation and frustration.

Paul told us,

> *Let all bitterness, wrath, anger, clamor, and evil speaking be put away from you, with all malice. And be kind to one another, tenderhearted, forgiving one another, just as God in Christ forgave you.* (Ephesians 4:31–32)

Manipulation is an evil tactic inspired by the devil. When we try to manage what our spouses think, we are being used by the devil! Christ did not manipulate His bride, the church, into doing what He wanted; He gave Himself to her completely. We must make the decision to extend grace and be kind and to seek the will of God in our disagreements, not just do what makes us feel good.

Another very effective tactic for manipulation is the "remember when you..." tactic. This method uses the past to affect the present. Some issue comes up and your spouse cannot "win" the argument, so he or she brings up some similar failure on your part from the past. The issue may have been resolved long ago, but he or she brings it up as a weapon. Both parties need to agree that what is past is past and what is settled is settled. Neither the past nor settled issues should be used as tools for manipulation.

There is also the "just look at you..." maneuver, in which one person brings up an obviously unrelated weakness in the other to weaken the other's position. In this case spouses use a point of vulnerability to get what they want. Neither of the two strategies is fair or healthy in a marriage. They show the desire to "win" rather than to pursue peace. Any attempt to use the weakness or past mistakes of the other opens a door through which the enemy is only too happy to enter.

Of course, there are many other forms and tactics of manipulation, but all of them devalue the other person by denying that spouse his or her opinion and place in the house. In every case, manipulation tries to influence the emotions of the other person by making him or her feel ashamed, rejected, or stupid. In the end the one who tries to manipulate the other is the one who loses.

When we cannot "trick" someone into doing what we want, we may resort to scaring him or her into it. This is intimidation.

INTIMIDATION
When we intimidate, we try to scare or threaten to get our way. If we cannot "trick" someone, we scare him. Intimidation can take many forms, either verbal or physical. It is usually the result of feeling that we have

lost control of a situation. Intimidation is a way to make a lot of noise to scare someone into line.

When people feel that they are losing control, they may resort to threats, sometimes saying things like, "If you don't come home now, I'm not responsible for my actions," or "If you don't do this or that, I'm going to take your name off the bank accounts." Intimidation may include belittling, threatening, name-calling, insulting, or even being physically violent, but the issue is always a need to control—and it is a form of abuse. Intimidation is a way in which we bully people to our advantage through fear.

> INTIMIDATION IS A WAY TO MAKE A LOT OF NOISE TO SCARE SOMEONE INTO LINE.

Fear is a powerful weapon of the enemy—one that keeps us from living in peace. It was fear that the enemy used to keep the nation of Israel out of the land that God promised to them. Where there should have been abundance, there was only the dryness of desert sand. That was not God's intention. It also is not God's intention for a husband or a wife to rule over a home by instilling fear.

Both men and women use intimidation by threatening abandonment. "If you don't do what I say, I'll just leave!" How can we ever live in peace if we rule by fear? We can't. A house ruled by fear is one that will never know peace or purpose. Fear, by its very nature, freezes people in their tracks. It caused Israel to wander in the wilderness for forty years. Intimidation also cuts at the trust and mutual submission that is at the heart of any relationship, especially a marriage. When we try to scare, we scar and tear away the foundation of the home. Intimidation, like manipulation, never works, and in the end it leaves everyone exhausted.

When we cannot trick or scare people, we then try to dominate them.

DOMINATION

Domination is an attempt to move someone out of his or her position. We might see domination more from men, but it is the province of both sexes. Domination is the use of our own position to force someone to agree with us. We have found that men try to hold 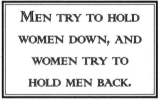 women down and women try to hold men back. Both are tactics of domination.

Jeannie: Sometimes men complain that their wives will not allow them to be the man that the women claim to have desired for so many years. The reality is that she has been in charge for so long that now it is hard for her to let go or share the control and responsibilities of the household. I know, because that was once my problem as well.

When we were first married, my husband was away from the home about twenty days out of the month. The children were used to seeing me control the day-to-day activities of the home, so when my husband came back home they treated him as a visitor instead of the head of the home. When he would come home and look into the refrigerator, they would run to me and say,

"Mama, he's in the refrigerator." But after my husband was home more of the time, he naturally began to take more responsibility in the house. At first I didn't want to let go of the past or my control. I held on to bitterness, saying, "If I let it go, he's gonna win; so I'm going to just hang on to it because I want to punish him. I want God to get him for what he did." However, as he got more involved at home, I began to trust him and watch him grow into his position. I stopped trying to dominate him and keep him out of his place.

At the same time, although some wives try to hold men back, some men try to hold women down.

Sometimes, when a woman begins to grow personally or professionally, her husband might feel that his position and power are being threatened. So when she goes back to school, he thinks she's trying to be smarter than him, or when she dresses up, he feels that she's dressing up for some other man. All of this is the result of insecurity.

There once was a couple in our church who wanted to start a construction business. The husband was very skillful in construction, and his wife was good at organization and communication. My husband advised the man to let his wife handle the financial component of the business and the communication with the clients, but the husband felt threatened and disregarded his advice. Without the wife doing what she could do best, the man was overwhelmed and the business failed. The pressure of the failure also ended their marriage. It was all because the husband did not trust his own wife to do what she was gifted to do in partnership with him. With this man it was all or nothing—and he ended up with nothing.

Men need to consider the advice from their wives rather than feel threatened by it. Their wives have been put alongside them for a reason. Who would better know the strengths and vulnerabilities of the husband than the wife? She is not trying to take the husband's place; she is trying to operate in her own place. Ask God to give you what works for your relationship, and to show you how to make it prosper and continually grow.

STOP THE BATTLE!

The control issue must stop. Each partner must allow the other to grow and become what God has gifted him or her to become. There needs to be *space* and *grace* in order for our partners to grow, and both are needed in the context of total transparency and honesty held together by trust. By far the biggest issue is, once again, communication. Husbands and wives should talk together and dream together, each encouraging the other toward his or her maximum potential. Finally, communication has to include communication with God through prayer. We should be praying for our marriage, family, mission, and purpose together. This leads all the parties in the house toward unity in the Spirit of God.

We *both* wanted our marriage enough to step aside for the other person. We *both* had to change and stop trying to win all the time. We have suffered some of the same control tactics and pitfalls that your marriage has, but we continue to grow—even with the writing of this book. We have come to trust and appreciate one another, feeling secure with and not having to try to control the other. As we have learned to communicate honestly, we have flourished in our roles. We pray that your house will find the same kind of trust and transparency that we are finding even with this writing. Nevertheless, the first one you must trust is God Himself, that He has put you together to build a strong and sane house together. He is in control!

WHAT WE ARE SAYING

Here are a few things that we have learned about the issue of control:

- Manipulation is trying to trick someone to your way of thinking.

- Intimidation is scaring someone into doing what you want him or her to do.

- Domination is trying to move someone out of his or her position in the house.

- Manipulation leads to anger and bitterness and the death of marriages and people.

- Intimidation and fear keep us out of God's promises.

- The key to stopping the battle for control is communication, including communication with God through prayer.

CHAPTER EIGHT

POWERING THE HOUSE
WITH THE
GLORY OF GOD

CHAPTER EIGHT

POWERING THE HOUSE
WITH THE
GLORY OF GOD

WHAT SHINES THROUGH THE WINDOWS
OF YOUR HOUSE?

Bishop: There is a crisis of ignorance in the church today regarding marriage and the family. I don't mean ignorance in the sense that we don't know there is a problem, but ignorance in the fact that we ignore the problem. We have too many families who are weak and falling apart, and as a result the church is unstable. The houses we build as individual families throughout the body of Christ are no stronger than those built by non-Christians. The church, the household of God, is a household of households—it is a family of families. The household of God is made up of our own individual households, so if we have a church filled with sane houses, we will have sane churches. The opposite is also true, that when the individual houses are crazy, the churches will be crazy, too. Therefore, we must respond by teaching and strengthening God's vision for marriage and the family.

Many churches offer romantic weekend retreats for couples to get away together to rekindle flames

IT TAKES MORE THAN ROMANTIC GETAWAYS AND BETTER COMMUNICATION SKILLS TO BUILD SOLID MARRIAGES.

of passion. Retreats offer warm fireplaces, soft lighting, and opportunities for intimacy without the children. Such retreats may teach married couples how to communicate with one another in more sensitive ways and are great for rekindling the old fires of passion and romance. However, regardless of how much wood you throw on the fire, the fire will eventually burn out! It will take more than romantic getaways and better communication skills to build solid marriages and families.

The houses we are building need an inexhaustible power source to sustain them. It's great to rekindle our romance and passion for our spouse, but there is another rekindling that must happen—a rekindling of passion for the presence of God in our marriage and households. The presence and glory of God allow us to keep the lights burning when challenges come. The presence and glory of God hold our houses together even when the world, the flesh, and the devil are trying to pull them apart. The glory and presence of God

> THE PRESENCE AND GLORY OF GOD HOLD OUR HOUSES TOGETHER EVEN WHEN THEY ARE BEING PULLED APART.

are an inexhaustible source of power for the sane and solid households we aspire to build. So we must learn how to fill our houses with the glory of God.

POWER IN THE HOUSE

Throughout biblical history, God has called men to build places of habitation for Him. He called Moses to build a tabernacle in the wilderness, so that He might *"dwell among them"* (Exodus 25:8). Later God caused Solomon, the son of David, to build Him a permanent temple in Jerusalem for the same purpose. (See 1 Chronicles 29.) In every case, when God called man to build Him a dwelling place, He filled it with His own manifest presence. The pattern was always the same: God gave direction to build a house; then, once it was built according to His instructions, He filled it with His glory. (See Exodus 40:33–34.)

Every house that God has ever built has the same source of power: His presence and glory. What exactly is this inexhaustible power source—the glory of God?

> *Yours, O LORD, is the greatness, the power and the glory, the victory and the majesty; for all that is in heaven and in earth is Yours; Yours*

*is the kingdom, O LORD, and You are exalted
as head over all. Both riches and honor come
from You, and You reign over all. In Your hand
is power and might; in Your hand it is to make
great and to give strength to all.*

(1 Chronicles 29:11–12)

The glory of God is the surpassing greatness of God *seen* by human eyes. Moses requested of God, *"Show me thy glory"* (Exodus 33:18 KJV). Glory is not a mere theological concept; it is something that can be seen. First Chronicles 29:11–12 is a psalm of praise lifted up at the final assembly of all the materials David gathered to build the place of God's habitation. David used words like *greatness, power, victory, majesty, riches, honor, reign, power, might,* and *strength* to describe the glory of God. Should the houses we build for God be any less?

When the glory of God fills the house, there is an empowering that takes place. It's the same for the houses we call marriage. God's glory, His manifest presence, shines through our marriage for the entire world to see. People notice the way a husband treats his wife. People see when a wife loves her husband as an equal partner in the house. People observe how children raised in a house filled with the presence of God respect their teachers in school. The world will see that we have our house in order and that we have peace and joy in the Holy Spirit. (See Romans 14:17.)

But how do we empower our houses with the glory of God? How do we manifest His presence through our homes? Let's look at an example. When Solomon finished building the great and glorious house for God on Mount Zion, it was filled with the presence of God:

> *And it came to pass when the priests came out of the Most Holy Place (for all the priests who were present had sanctified themselves, without keeping to their divisions)...indeed it came to pass, when the trumpeters and singers were as one...in praising and thanking the LORD... saying: "For He is good, for His mercy endures forever," that the house, the house of the LORD, was filled with a cloud....When Solomon had finished praying, fire came down from heaven and consumed the burnt offering and the sacrifices; and the glory of the LORD filled the temple.... When all the children of Israel saw how the fire came down, and the glory of the LORD on the temple, they bowed their faces to the ground on the pavement, and worshiped and praised the LORD.*   (2 Chronicles 5:11, 13; 7:1, 3)

This was a house that was filled with the glory of God. Remember that we said marriage is "the coming together of two people who desire to build something of eternal value that brings glory to God." If we are to see our houses filled with the presence and glory of God, we will have to follow the same pattern. To build a sane house that brings glory to God requires four things: *obedience, unity, dedication,* and *sacrifice.*

POWER THROUGH OBEDIENCE

There is nothing more important to God than obedience. God desires obedience more than ritual or sacrifice. (See 1 Samuel 15:22.) Our obedience is the proof that we are paying attention to what God says. When God wanted to build a house, He gave careful instructions as to how to build it and what materials to use. He told Moses,

> *And let them make Me a sanctuary, that I may dwell among them. According to all that I show you, that is, the pattern of the tabernacle and the pattern of all its furnishings, just so you shall make it.* (Exodus 25:8–9)

Everything in the house that God built pointed to something eternal about God. The order of the house reflected the order of heaven itself.

We have been talking about the God-reflecting order in the households we are building. But the glory and power of God will not fill a house that is not built in accordance with His instructions. If you wanted to build a new house and the contractor you hired ignored your blueprints, you would not move into the house. Why? Because the house would not suit your purpose—it would not be what you wanted. In the same way, God will not move into a house when we ignore His instructions for building. Following those

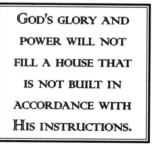

GOD'S GLORY AND POWER WILL NOT FILL A HOUSE THAT IS NOT BUILT IN ACCORDANCE WITH HIS INSTRUCTIONS.

instructions is obedience, and obedience is necessary if we want God to fill and empower our house.

POWER THROUGH UNITY

We said before that marriage is oneness, but unity or oneness seems to run against human nature. To be in unity means that we are moving in the same direction toward the same thing. In order for George and Jeannie Bloomer to move together in one direction, we have to stop going in our own directions and move as one. We have separate roles within our marriage, yes, but only one focus: bringing the glory of God into the house.

There must be a single focus or purpose that binds husband and wife and the rest of the family together. It's similar to our times of corporate worship. When we are in a worship service, there is a pulse or a beat that causes the whole congregation to move as one, to clap hands or sing together. We may bring a variety of concerns and understandings and backgrounds when we come together in the service, but we are all singing the same tune and moving to the same beat. We all have a singular focus: the worthiness of God to be praised.

It was when all the priests were praising God *"as one"* (2 Chronicles 5:13) that the glory of God filled the house. The Bible says that they gathered in that single focus *"without keeping to their divisions"* (v. 11). In other words, they may have served in different places in the house, but they were all focused on the same thing.

All that they did was an act of worship that ushered in the presence of God. Like those priests, a husband and wife play different roles in their household, but both of them need to be focused on the presence and glory of God. A husband's covering leadership is his act of worship, and a wife performs the functions of her "sub-mission" as her act of worship. The thing that allows them to be in unity is their single focus on bringing the presence of God into the house.

There is only one source of unity for sane and solid houses, and that is the reality of the presence of Jesus Christ. When Jesus prayed for us, He asked the Father that

> ...the glory which You gave Me I have given them, that they may be one just as We are one: I in them, and You in Me; that they may be made perfect in one, and that the world may know that You have sent Me, and have loved them as You have loved Me. (John 17:22–23)

We are able to be one because we have one focus: Jesus. Jesus was one with the Father because He was focused on what the Father was doing and what would bring Him glory. George and Jeannie Bloomer are held in unity because we are one in Jesus, not because we agree on everything. Jesus is the backdrop for everything we do, from paying bills to raising children.

For a house to be in unity, it must have a single focus on the presence of God. However, although unity is a matter of focus or purpose, dedication is a matter of ownership.

POWER THROUGH DEDICATION

When we dedicate a person or place to God, we transfer ownership of that person or place to Him. Dedication is a public notice that something is set apart for God alone. In 2 Chronicles 6, Solomon prayed a prayer of dedication for the house of God. He publicly declared that this was God's property.

When we dedicate children, we are transferring them into the kingdom of God. What God owns, God takes care of. We are saying that from that time on, they are God's to do with as He pleases. We do not take them back again after the dedication service. In the same way, our households must be dedicated to God; ownership of the house must be transferred to Him, to do with it as He pleases.

The households and families we are building are not multipurpose buildings. They cannot be used for our purpose *and* for God's any more than a consecrated church building would be used for worship on Sunday and a brothel on Monday. When we dedicate our house to God, we give Him ownership.

When our house becomes the rightful property of God, we cease operating in our own power and look to God. In his prayer of dedication, Solomon asked that the Lord hear the needs presented in His house. (See 2 Chronicle 6:19–20.) When our house becomes

God's house, we stop keeping score when we mess up. Because it's God's house, there is grace to restore us.

Jeannie and I have been married now for more than eighteen years, and we have found that marriage comes with challenges beyond our ability to handle. Now, our challenges may be different from yours. Some couples may not have enough money; maybe some can't decide what to do with the money they have. And there are times when, despite our best efforts, our kids make mistakes and get into trouble. There will be other times when accidents or tragedies happen that we can do nothing about. But in all these times we remember that God owns the house, and we can look to Him when the bank account is empty. It's God's house when we are blessed, and it's still God's house when it seems to be crashing down around us.

> WHEN OUR HOUSE BECOMES GOD'S HOUSE, WE STOP KEEPING SCORE WHEN WE MESS UP.

When our house truly becomes God's house, both we and God are at rest. Solomon prayed, *"Now therefore, arise, O LORD God, to Your resting place, You and the ark of Your strength"* (2 Chronicles 6:41). God will not fill with His glory a house that does not belong to Him. If we are to see the glory of God fill and empower our houses, then we must hand over ownership to Him.

POWER THROUGH SACRIFICE

Sacrifice is not a very popular concept these days. Sacrifice hurts because it involves the death of flesh. We are more likely to try to save our skin than offer it up.

But sacrifice is the key to the glory and presence of God filling our houses. Notice it was when the fire of God came down and consumed the sacrifice that the glory of God filled the temple. The Bible says, *"When Solomon had finished praying, fire came down from heaven and consumed the burnt offering and the sacrifices; and the glory of the LORD filled the temple"* (2 Chronicles 7:1). The "glory cloud" that filled the temple was the smoke of burning flesh on the altar. The glory of God will also fill our houses when we put our flesh on the altar and invite God to consume it.

When we talk about putting our flesh on the altar, we are saying that there is something more important than our feeling good or having our own way. Putting our flesh on the altar means that we choose to set aside our own will and do what honors God. Notice that God never demands sacrifices from us; they have to be *offered.* We offer ourselves sacrificially when we refuse to allow our flesh to be in charge. We offer ourselves when we extend grace and understanding to our spouse. We offer ourselves when we choose to do the God-honoring thing instead of the convenient thing. We must offer our flesh on the altar if we are to see the glory of God filling our houses. Each offering brings a sweet smelling-aroma to heaven.

THE HOUSE THAT JESUS BUILT

All we have said about filling the house with the glory and power of God may seem difficult to accomplish, but once we have decided to go for the glory of God, we no longer depend on our ability. Jesus is the ultimate builder of our houses.

> *Now, therefore, you are no longer strangers and foreigners, but fellow citizens with the saints and members of the household of God, having been built on the foundation of the apostles and prophets, Jesus Christ Himself being the chief corner stone, in whom the whole building, being fitted together, grows into a holy temple in the Lord, in whom you also are being built together for a dwelling place of God in the Spirit.* (Ephesians 2:19–22)

Jesus is the *"corner stone"* who holds us together. He has fulfilled all the elements required for filling His own house with the glory of God.

- *Obedience:* Jesus *"learned obedience by the things which He suffered"* for us (Hebrews 5:8).

- *Unity:* Jesus knew unity in being *"one"* with the Father (John 10:30).

- *Dedication:* Jesus was dedicated to the purposes of God in that He did only what He saw the Father doing. (See John 5:19.)

- *Sacrifice:* And greatest of all, Jesus offered Himself as the Lamb of God on the altar of sacrifice. (See John 10:15–18.)

Jesus has not only fulfilled all the criteria, but He has also become the source of grace and power for us to do the same. Because Jesus has gone before us to empower us, we have the grace to cover the many times when we blow it. We need to remember that we are "growing" into a house filled with the glory of God. We are going to make mistakes; we will get angry and yell at one another and forget to honor the others in the house. But we will continue to grow into a house filled with the glory of God one choice at a time, remembering that when we build a house for the glory of God, He will fill it with His own power and presence.

> [Lord] *that Your eye may be open toward this house day and night, toward the place of which You have said that You would put Your name there, to listen to the prayer which Your servant shall pray toward this place....Now therefore arise, O LORD God, to Your resting place, You and the ark of Your might; let Your priests, O LORD God, be clothed with salvation and let Your godly ones rejoice in what is good.*
>
> (2 Chronicles 6:20, 41 NASU)

WHAT WE ARE SAYING

Here are a few of the things we have learned about building a house for the glory of God:

- The church, the household of faith, is only as strong as the houses that comprise it.

- The power supply for the houses we build is the presence of God.

- The glory of God shines through the houses we build.

CHAPTER NINE

CRAZY HOUSE OR
SANE HOUSE

CHAPTER NINE

CRAZY HOUSE OR SANE HOUSE

WHAT KIND OF HOUSE ARE YOU BUILDING?

In the next few pages, we will recapture some of the truths from each facet of the houses we are building. As you read through this chapter, you will visit each phase of your own house and be challenged to compare what you have to what we have observed. We advise anyone who is married or contemplating marriage to go through this chapter, honestly inspecting each area of the house. This is where the hard work and the grace of God begin.

You will need a separate piece of paper to complete this chapter. We suggest that you keep these papers in a notebook of some kind so that you can go back and compare your initial answers with the progress you are making. All of these questions are meant to lead you into more dialogue rather than to short answers. It is our desire to help you bring any problems to the surface so that you can deal with them honestly and build a strong and sane house.

LAYING THE FOUNDATION

What kind of foundation does your house have?

- *Anything built without purpose and vision is doomed to fail.*

On a piece of paper, each party, without comparing notes, should write down his or her five-year plan (for your life, marriage, career, family). How do you see your life together unfolding in the next five years? You will need to include at least the areas mentioned below on your paper. Add any other areas that involve major lifelong concerns within your marriage. (This is probably the hardest part of the chapter!)

Goals for spiritual life

Goals for your marriage

Goals for personal improvement

Goals for finances

Goals for career advancement

Goals for your spouse

- *Marriage is a calling to be one in purpose and vision.*

After you both have completed the assessment, compare notes. Note the differences, discuss them, and begin to write a separate five-year plan that reflects the plans of both of you. Discuss how each of you might help the other to meet his or her personal goals.

- *You cannot stay where you are and respond to the calling of God.*

What are some of the things that surprised you in your spouse's five-year plan? What kinds of changes will be required of you in order for you to be in agreement with your spouse?

- *God has called you together to bring glory to Him.*

What would you like your grandchildren to say about your marriage? How do you and your spouse reflect the love and character of God through your marriage?

- *Courtship is a time of preparation, not a test drive.*

Talk about the kind of courtship you have now or had prior to marriage. Did you date (test drive) many prospective mates? What were you looking for in a spouse?

- *Parents have the right and responsibility to take part in courtship.*

Did you get married with your parents' blessing and participation? How much time do you spend or did you spend with your parents prior to marriage?

- *Courtship is serious business that affects us for life.*

What things do you wish you had known about your spouse before you got married that you found out afterward? What would you tell others to help them find out about their prospective spouses before they get married?

- *Communication begins when we begin communicating.*

How often do you talk to your spouse about more than the bills? What do you talk about most of the time when it's your turn to talk?

- *People need to feel as though they are heard.*

Name one or two things that your spouse has told you about his or her concerns in the last few days. Where is your spouse happy, and where is he or she unhappy?

- *To resolve conflict, we need stop trying to prove that we are right.*

In what areas of your life do you always have to be right? Why? What ongoing areas of disagreement do you have with your spouse where you are now willing to listen to him or her fully rather than being right?

- *Every family and every individual needs some sacred space.*

Where is your sacred space in the house? Where do you feel comfortable? Where is your spouse's sacred space?

BUILDING THE HOUSE

- *Husbands are to provide physical, financial, and emotional stability for the house.*

Who paid the bills in the home where you grew up? What kind of emotional environment was there in the home? What kind of husband and father was in the house, and what kind would you like to see in your house?

- *Husbands are to be managing but equal partners in the house.*

Where do you feel like a partner in your house, and where do you not? Who does what in your household? (List regular areas of responsibility.) Where, if anywhere, do you feel left out in your house?

- *Husbands are to provide headship, not a dictatorship.*

What is the difference between headship and dictatorship? Which one exists in your house?

- *Husbands who don't cover wives force them to cover themselves.*

Wives, where do you feel as though you are covering for your husband instead of him covering you? Where do you feel unsafe? Husbands, do you hear your wife?

- *"Sub-mission" means that the wife is in order on the same mission as her husband.*

Where do you both seem to be working together, and where are you going in different directions?

- *Submission is not submersion.*

Wives, where do you feel overwhelmed or smothered? Is there a place or an issue where you feel you don't have any voice? Husbands, do you hear your wife?

- *There are not two heads of a household, one natural and one spiritual.*

Where are you both leading each other spiritually, and how? How much do you pray together? How can you each pray for each other right now? Do it!

- *Husbands need to invest in the gifts and abilities of their wives.*

How have both of you invested in the gifts and delights of your partner? What is it that he or she really likes to do, and how can you take part in it? Be definite in your answer, and make a plan right now to follow through.

- *The first thing that changes in our marriages is our understanding of ourselves.*

How have you personally changed since you got married or since you began seriously thinking about getting married? Reveal one thing that you learned about yourself since you got married that you didn't know before.

- *Marriage is a process that molds and shapes us into who we really are.*

How have each of you molded and adapted to the other since your relationship began? What have you learned about the real person of your mate?

- *There must be a respect of the marriage relationship within the family.*

Do either of you ever discuss your marriage with anyone in your family? Do you ever feel outnumbered by your spouse's family? When?

- *Children don't cause marital problems; worry about children does.*

If you have children, what do you worry about the most? What keeps you up at night? If you don't have children, what are your biggest concerns about having them, either naturally or by adoption? Do your children respect your mate? Why or why not?

POWER IN THE HOUSE

- *Manipulation is trying to trick someone into your way of thinking.*

Manipulation is like psychological warfare in the house. Where do you sometimes feel tricked into something? When and how have you been tricked?

- *Intimidation is scaring someone into doing what you want him or her to do.*

Have you ever threatened physical abuse or been threatened by physical harm by your spouse? Have you ever threatened to leave your spouse?

- **Domination** *is trying to move someone out of his or her position in the house.*

Husbands and wives can sometimes crush one another with words and attitudes. Have you ever felt crushed by your spouse? Do you ever hold out on your spouse in some way? Why?

- *Manipulation leads to anger and bitterness and the death of marriages and people.*

As you think about the past, are there any areas of darkness where something remains unsettled? Do you feel anger toward your spouse for anything? Tell him or her what it is and how you feel, then forgive and release your spouse now that you have been heard. (He or she does not have to ask for forgiveness for you to do so.)

- *Intimidation and fear keep us out of God's promises.*

What have you been afraid to reach for as a couple? Why? What do you think God has to say about that area? (For example, some couples may be afraid to have children because of abuse in their childhood home.) What is fear keeping you from?

- *The power supply for the houses we build is the presence of God.*

Is the prevailing feeling in your home one of peace or frenzy? Discuss any area where you lack peace with your spouse, and give it over to God.

- *Obedience, unity, dedication, and sacrifice are the criteria for building houses to the glory of God.*

Where do you sense that God is taking you in your marriage, personal life, and relationship to Him? What are you willing to put on the altar to get to where God is leading you?

Now that you have gone through this whole book and this assessment chapter, what have you learned about yourself and your spouse? We suggest that you revisit these questions and your notebooks on a regular basis to appreciate your own growth and God's grace.

Now look into your spouse's face and pray blessing over him or her as you each take your place in a sane house.

A FINAL WORD TO THE
MATURING HOUSE

A FINAL WORD TO THE MATURING HOUSE

W hat blueprint are you committed to following to build a long-lasting, successful union with your mate, and what building material are you using to ensure a firm foundation for your home? As couples, many times we think that as long as we're both saved, our marriage will be just fine. We quote the Scripture, *"Be ye not unequally yoked together with unbelievers"* (2 Corinthians 6:14 KJV), and assume that as long as we are married to a believer, our marriage will just flow on. However, both partners bring different levels of maturity to the marriage—levels that will grow with time and patience. Personal salvation is not a safeguard against trials and temptations, nor is it the guarantee of a life of "happily ever after."

Two people who love God and are good people do not necessarily have all the ingredients for a good marriage. Oftentimes when couples we know divorce, we are shocked and say, "But they're such nice people." Many of us know "nice people" who find it virtually impossible to live together, to agree, or to come together as one as the Bible commands. In the final analysis, houses are held together more by friendship between the partners than by passion between lovers. Choosing a partner who is spiritually mature and shares your vision for future growth increases your chances for a happy marriage—a marriage where two people are willing, despite differences, to fight through any trials that the marriage will encounter.

Giving of ourselves to our spouses is a sign of maturity. It is the mature person who sees the dirty dishes in the sink and does them without waiting for his or her partner to do them. Both individuals should be willing to give of themselves and bend a little every now and then to meet the needs of the other individual. Then, as our marriages mature, we begin to see the needs of the house and respond without waiting for a standing ovation. We serve our spouses and at the same time ourselves. The two are one flesh, and no person hates his or her own flesh. (See Ephesians 5:29.) As we grow in grace, our eyes will be turned toward our partners in marriage to see their needs before our own. We will extend grace when they slip on a banana peel or burn the beans. Grace is the indication of true maturity and growth in the houses we are building.

As we grow together, let us show love, display joy, seek peace, endure frailties through long-suffering, show gentleness, have faith amid trials to pull the family together, and exhibit meekness and temperance instead of immediately flaring up when differences arise. (See Galatians 5:22–23.) These are the much-needed building materials for cohesiveness within our homes. They will be the difference between a crazy house and a sane house.

We pray that you continue to build your sane house to the glory of God.

OTHER POWERFUL ooks

from Whitaker House

This Is War
George Bloomer

Just when you think you're gaining new revelation from God and developing fresh intimacy with Him, the devil comes to deny you
of all your progress. Fellow warrior George
Bloomer describes how you can effectively
silence satan's roar and quash his assault.
Soon the devil's oppression of your mind and
spirit will be history!

ISBN: 0-88368-674-0 • Trade • 160 pages

When Loving You Is Wrong
George Bloomer

We were created as relational beings. However, we often find ourselves in many
imperfect relationships. George Bloomer
shares some important lessons on developing
wholesome, fulfilling relationships. As you
discover how much God loves you, you will
also recognize that the best relationship of all
is intimacy with Him.

ISBN: 0-88368-504-3 • Trade • 188 pages

POWERFUL VIDEOS
by George Bloomer

But the Tomb Is Empty • ISBN: 0-88368-680-5 • UPC: 6-30809-68680-0

Cockroaches and Bootleg Preachers (2-video set)
ISBN: 0-88368-734-8 • UPC: 6-30809-68734-0

Crossing Over • ISBN: 0-88368-733-X • UPC: 6-30809-68733-3

The Hem of His Garment • ISBN: 0-88368-196-X • UPC: 6-30809-68196-6

I'm Not Who I Told You I Was
ISBN: 0-88368-676-7 • UPC: 6-30809-68676-3

It's Mess That Makes You • ISBN: 0-88368-740-2 • UPC: 6-30809-68740-1

It's the Law • ISBN: 0-88368-678-3 • UPC: 6-30809-68678-7

Let's Go to the Other Side • ISBN: 0-88368-215-X • UPC: 6-30809-68215-4

Look Who I'm with Now • ISBN: 0-88368-732-1 • UPC: 6-30809-68732-6

Man in the Mirror • ISBN: 0-88368-739-9 • UPC: 6-30809-68739-5

Mining Your Mind • ISBN: 0-88368-736-4 • UPC: 6-30809-68736-4

No Weapon • ISBN: 0-88368-731-3 • UPC: 6-30809-68731-9

Now How Are You Going to Get Home?
ISBN: 0-88368-679-1 • UPC: 6-30809-68679-4

Questions and Answers with George Bloomer
ISBN: 0-88368-738-0 • UPC: 6-30809-68738-8

Warning: Angels in Charge • ISBN: 0-88368-677-5 • UPC: 6-30809-68677-0

What's in the Bag? • ISBN: 0-88368-737-2 • UPC: 6-30809-68737-1

Where Eagles Fly • ISBN: 0-88368-201-X • UPC: 6-30809-68201-7

Witchcraft in the Pews • ISBN: 0-88368-735-6 • UPC: 6-30809-68735-7

You Dropped Me, God Caught Me
ISBN: 0-88368-232-X • UPC: 6-30809-68232-1

OTHER POWERFUL Books
from Whitaker House

Understanding the Purpose and Power of Men
Dr. Myles Munroe

Today, the world is sending out conflicting signals about what it means to be a man. Many men are questioning who they are and what roles they fulfill in life—as a male, a husband, and a father. Best-selling author Myles Munroe examines cultural attitudes toward men and discusses the purpose God has given them. Discover the destiny and potential of the man as he was meant to be.

ISBN: 0-88368-725-9 • Trade • 224 pages

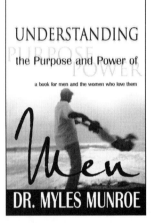

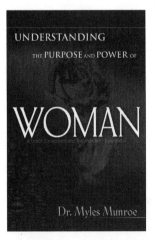

Understanding the Purpose and Power of Woman
Dr. Myles Munroe

To live successfully in the world, women need to know what role they play. They need a new awareness of who they are, and new skills to meet today's challenges. Myles Munroe helps women to discover who they are. Whether you are a woman or a man, married or single, this book will help you to understand the woman as she was meant to be.

ISBN: 0-88368-671-6 • Trade • 208 pages